WARTI1
SCHOOLD
IN BOSTON

First outing to Skegness after the war;
with Noel and Ivor Holgate

PAUL MOULD

First published in 1996

PUBLISHED BY
PAUL MOULD

Copyright © Paul Mould 1996

ISBN: 0 9528708 0 0

PRINTED IN GREAT BRITAIN BY
GEMINI PRINTERS LTD.

CONTENTS

TO AUSTIN DAVIES
who was the first to insist that I should write this book
but died, before it was completed.

3rd. SEPTEMBER,1939

"The day war broke out...my missus said to me...what are you going to do about it?" Robb Wilton helped everyone to see the funny side of it but no one was laughing that Sunday morning, when Neville Chamberlain made his broadcast.

Our neighbour, Mrs. Burton, broke the news, as even on a Sunday our wireless was never switched on until evening. My reaction did not match that of my parents, as I had no conception then of the change to everyone's life that would be made that day. As a five year old still settling to life in the infants at Staniland School, war was just something that our gang did with the William's gang.

Mrs. Burton was naturally concerned as she had two sons, who would soon be old enough for conscription and her husband's health had never recovered from the effects of gas in the First World War.

My parents greeted the announcement with foreboding, for like millions of others they had lived through one war and, after just twenty-one years, they dreaded the prospect of facing another conflict that promised to be even worse. My mother had joined other girls in seeing troop trains waiting in Boston station full of young lads glimpsing the last friendly faces, before taking their place at the front in France.

My father had enlisted in the Royal Flying Corps at the age of seventeen; trained as a navigator at Farnborough and finished the war in hospital.

Contingency plans had been made in advance and the Borough of Boston was part of the North Midland Region, whose Commisioner was Lord Trent.

The Deputy Regional Commissioner was Principal H.A.S. Wortley and the County A.R.P. Controller was H.C. Marris.

The Sub-Controller for Boston was Chief Constable Leonard Johnson.

A booklet was quickly published telling people what precautions to take and what to do in all emergencies. The price was 3d. The expert knowledge of Sergeant J.R. Livock and Chief Fire Officer F.F. Carter assured the accuracy and soundness of the advice.

The booklet described the air raid warning as a fluctuating or warbling blast on electric sirens of two minutes duration and the raiders past, which soon became known as the all clear, was a continuous blast for two minutes.

There was a general fear and expectation that Hitler would use gas and it was arranged that in the event of a gas alarm wardens would use hand rattles and to cancel a gas warning they would use handbells.

Sirens were situated on the Municipal Buildings in West Street, Thompsons Mill in Spilsby Road, Fisher Clarks in Norfolk Street, Stinson's Garage in London Road, the Woodville Road Pumping Station, Witham Bank and the Dock.

The advice on what action to take on hearing an air raid warning was to stay indoors, if at home and, if in the street, either go home, if within easy reach, or to a public air raid shelter.

If in a motor vehicle, stop at the first suitable place without blocking the highway; switch off headlights but leave on side and rear lights; leave vehicle unlocked but remove any valuables; park in open space away from buildings, if carrying petrol, explosives or anything dangerous or inflammable.

For horse-drawn vehicles the advice was to unharness the horses, tie them by the halter lead not the reins to the rear of the vehicle not to lamp posts or railings, fasten the halter below the hub of the wheel and fasten the vehicle with skid breaks or chains.

There was no need to put on your respirator immediately the sirens sounded but it was imperative if you heard the gas warning rattles or if you smelt gas.

Everyone was issued with a respirator but they remained the property of the Government and there was a charge, if you either damaged or lost it. They were generally referred to as gas masks and they were issued in a box but most people bought a canvass holder that could be strung round the shoulder.

We were instructed to get used to them by wearing them regularly for a short time. At school we had lessons in taking them on and off as quickly as possible without damaging them. The booklet advised for them to be kept in a cool dry clean place; to be carried at all times; never to be exposed to strong light, heat, intense cold or moisture and once a month they should be removed from the box and aired for twenty-four hours to restore the shape of the face piece.

Such was the fear of gas attacks at the start of the war that everyone obeyed these instructions conscientiously and you would no more leave the house without your gas mask as you would without your trousers.

We all learned about the different gases. Tear gases were harmless but they could be used to cause panic, as they were similar to the more harmful blister gases. The sore eyes soon recovered, after doning your respirator.

Nose gases were worse, as the symptons (headache, toothache, sneezing, sore throat and chest) were slow to clear, even when wearing your gas mask but you must leave it on until they abate, then go home, leave your clothes outside and drink plenty of liquids.

Lung gases were deadly but the gas masks gave
complete protection and they could be detected by the smell
of chlorine and the coughing and choking effect.
Worst of all were the blister gases, for example mustard
gas, as they gave no immediate symptons but, although not
deadly, they caused casualties and disorganised medical
services. They could be vapour or liquid and in either form
they caused blisters on the skin, so the gas mask did not
give full protection. Mustard gas smelt of onions,
garlic or horse-radish and the quicker-acting Lewisite gas
smelt of geraniums. Their effect lasted much longer and
anything contaminated by them should not be touched nor
even approached.

The all clear usually followed no more than a few hours
after an air raid but it could be days after a gas raid, before
it was safe to venture out; so people were advised to stock
up a cellar or the ground floor room with the fewest windows
with the following: food in tins, water in stone jars or bottles,
a tin opener, torches, books, papers, wireless, table games,
sanitary utensils, first-aid box and a respirator for each
person.

The lucky ones had brick blast-walls outside their
windows but others were advised to build two and a half feet
walls of sandbags or boxes containing earth, sand or ashes.
window glass should be covered with cellophane or
adhesive tape to avoid flying splinters caused by blast. It
was a good idea to have an emergency frame made with
wire netting and covered with a blanket and keep it handy in
case a window should be blown in.

Most of the bombs dropped were incendiaries and did
not explode but burst into flames on impact. They were
designed to penetrate ordinary roofs and rest between the
roof and the ceiling or in a bedroom. They would throw off
white-hot molten particles for about two minutes then they
would burn for fifteen minutes. In case one landed on your
roof it was advisable to clear the space under the roof of all
inflammable material and provide easy access; making

sure that trap-doors would move freely and a ladder was handy to reach it. A coat of thick lime-wash on the rafters would help to check the fire.

A good habit for all householders was to fill baths and buckets with water as soon as the alarm sounded, in case the mains were damaged in the raid and water was needed urgently. Most houses had at least one stirrup hand pump readily available.

The recommendations concerning fire-fighting apply just the same today. Keep doors and windows closed, as a draught will make a fire larger: a closed door will confine a fire to one room for a considerable time.

If you are trapped in a burning building, you are safer in a room protected by a closed door than on a staircase or in a passage. Movement in a room on fire is safer, if you keep as close to the floor as possible. You will also see much better. When moving across a floor or down stairs, which have been weakened by fire, keep close to the walls, where the rafters are strongest. Always come down stairs feet first.

If searching a burning building, always start at the top and work to the comparative safety of the lower floors. Never alow a person whose clothes are on fire to remain standing, as flames rise: lay them down and smother the flames with a coat or a carpet.

Many a life was saved, because people took notice of these instructions, which were largely common sense. It would be a good idea to make people aware today of the basic precautions and emergency routines to adopt in case of fire.

Air raid shelters sprung up like mushrooms in those early months of the war. Our playground at school shrunk, as shelters were built at the sides. They each had a large letter painted onto them and we all knew which one was allocated to our class.

When the siren sounded, while we were at school, we were trained to remain calm and line up in twos outside the classroom and wait for the teacher to take us to our shelter.

At home, when the dreaded "moaning minnie" sounded, the lucky ones crawled into their Anderson shelters, which often doubled as dining tables, while the majority dived under the kitchen table or down the cellar in the older houses. If caught in the street, too far from home, there were forty-six public shelters in the Borough of Boston to choose from.

There were six on Bargate Green, three in Brown's Yard, behind the New Theatre, two each at Buoy Yard, Shodfriars Hall, Bargate End, Norfolk Street, Thorold Street, Tawney Street and Soulby's Cellar and one each at Market Place, near Lloyd's Bank, 36, Market Place, Morris's Cellar on the Bridge foot, Reynold's Cellar, Labour Club, Fydell House, 120, High Street, Pulvertoft Lane, Fydell Crescent, Russell Square, Bond Street (Malt House), Station Path, Carlton Road, Sleaford Road, Hospital Bridge, Bargate Bridge, Moulders (Bargate), Silver Street (Gratton's Yard), Pump Square, Dolphin Lane, Burgess's Pitt, Wesleyan Church in Red Lion Street and the General Hospital.

Our local shelter was at the top of Pulvertoft Lane and at the start of the war we felt safer joining others there, rather than staying at home. Most of the raids were in the evening or during the night and you knew better what was happening, if you were in a shelter, for wardens and police were popping in and out at intervals.

The time passed more quickly in the company of twenty or thirty neighbours and fear subsided, as you listened to various fragments of conversation. Both the beer and camaraderie were transfered from the public houses into the shelters. We were often entertained by Mrs. Butler and Mrs. Simpson dancing up and down the central aisle, armed with a pint jug of ale but I can never remember them spilling a drop. They followed "Knees Up Mother Brown" with "Bless 'Em All" and everyone joined in.

As the months went by and the German planes were obviously passing over Boston to more important targets, people became braver and chose to ignore the sirens but once or twice an odd enemy plane would be returning home with bombs still loaded and they dropped them on Boston, probably aiming for the Docks or Railway. After these rare occasions, the shelters were again full for a few weeks and the songs suffered another rendering.

Conscription for men between the ages of eighteen and forty-one started immediately but there were several reserved occupations and the medicals were comprehensive with quite a few turned down for armed service.

In 1941, when the position looked desperate, women were conscripted and the reserved occupations for men were reviewed and the medical qualifications were relaxed. Women were placed in one of the armed forces or the Land Army. Many of those in the Land Army came to Lincolnshire, some from miles away, and they staid here after the war, either because they preferred the countryside or because they married a local lad.

In some cases they lived on the farms but others lived in hostels and today you still hear older people refer to the Leverton Village Hall, which now houses the Three Horseshoes, as the Land Army Hostel.

BEVERAGES.

TEA (Freshly brewed for each person)	per cup 2d.
	per pot 3d. per person
COFFEE	per cup 2d. and 3d.
COCOA	per cup 2d.
BOVRIL	per cup 4d.
OXO	per cup 2d.
HORLICK'S MALTED MILK	per glass 4d.
(with milk)	„ 6d.
GLASS OF MILK	per glass 2d.
MINERALS	per bottle 3d.

All Bread and Cakes served in our Cafe are made in our own Electrical Bakery.

COLD MEATS, FISH, &c.

HAM	per plate 6d. and 9d.
HAM & TONGUE	1/-
TONGUE	1/-
SALMON	9d.
CRAYFISH	9d.
CRAB	9d.
PORK PIE	per portion 8d.

FRUIT, &c.

FRUIT SALAD	per plate 8d.
FRUIT	„ 6d.

ICES.

STRAWBERRY	3d. each
VANILLA	3d. each
(With cream)	6d. each

CAKES, &c.

FANCY CAKES & PASTRIES	1½d. each
CUSTARDS	2d. „
SAUSAGE ROLLS	2d. „
BUTTERED SCONE	2d. „
BUTTERED TEA CAKE	4d. „
TOASTED TEA CAKE	5d. „

If you liked the Cakes served in Cafe why not take a few home? They can be purchased downstairs.

SUNDRIES.

EGGS (Boiled)	4d. each
„ Poached on Toast	7d. „
„ 2 „	10d.
BEANS ON TOAST	7d.
BREAD & BUTTER (white or brown)	per plate 3d. & 6d.
TOAST (dry)	per round 1½d.
„ (buttered)	2½d.
ROLL & BUTTER	3d.
CHEESE	per portion 2d.
PRESERVES	per jar 3d.
HAM SANDWICH	3d. each
TONGUE SANDWICH	4d. „

1939 Menu for Mould's Cafe at 17a, West Street

BILLETS AND BULLETS

Soon after the start of the war all houses were visited to ascertain the possibility of billeting soldiers or airmen. A good excuse was required, if you had an unused bedroom and refused to billet one or two servicemen. Most people were only too pleased to help and many life-long friendships were forged as a result. The following letter appeared in the Boston edition of the Lincolnshire Standard in 1992, written by Don Knight of 76, Larkdown, Wantage, Oxon:

" 1992 marks the 50th. anniversary of the year I went to Boston. It was early January and I had been in the R.A.F. for one whole week. In mid-afternoon some two hundred airmen arrived at Boston station, after a meandering train journey from Cardington in Bedfordshire.

There being no R.A.F. camp at Boston, we were billeted on families around the town. Two of us eventually found ourselves back at the station having carried our kit- bags to an address on a housing estate somewhere to the south-east of the town only to discover our intended landlady had gone away.

It was dark when we arrived back at the station but an R.A.F. corporal knew of an old lady, who sometimes took in airmen and so we met Mrs. Blackamore, a widowed grandmother, who took us in, warmed us, fed us and looked after us marvellously for the next two monthS. Each day, including Sundays, we paraded outside a small chapel in memorable Liquorpond Street, where we were taught to march to and fro and in step. The chapel was used for lectures and other mysteries of R.A.F. life.

It was a cold, snowy winter and most of our time was spent in our Station Street billet with an occasional parade to Boston Stump. Evenings were spent writing home or polishing our badges and buttons ready for the next day. Any night life in Boston was not for us on two shillings a day.

We lived happily with Mrs. Blackamore, who worked wonders with the rations she got for us. I don't remember much about her family, except for a granddaughter called Thora and she had a sister, who was a schoolteacher, who lived nearby and looked in often.

There were also a married couple related to Mrs. Blackamore, who ran a cake shop close to the top end of Liquorpond Street, where we took our morning break. They were very popular with all the airmen.

I do not recall much of Boston and I have not had cause to visit the area in all the years since the war.   Perhaps it is time I took a nostalgic trip but I bet it would not be easy these days to march two hundred airmen up and down Liquorpond Street."

I was very interested and pleased, when I saw Don Knight's letter, for the popular couple with the cake shop were my parents and Mrs. Blackamore, whom he remembered with affection, was my grandmother. Unfortunately she died in 1943, when she fell backwards down the stairs and also my cousin Thora, whom he mentioned, died in Canada several years ago.

He was only in Boston for two months and it was winter but, had he been here in the spring and summer, he could have enjoyed the bandstand concerts, that were organised by the P.S.A. (Pleasant Sunday Afternoon) in the Central Park to entertain the forces and civilians. Some soldiers and airmen joined in the proceedings; one particular favourite still remembered by many today was Drill Sergeant Leathers, who always sang "Begin the Beguine" and finished with "The Donkey Serenade". If you closed your eyes you would have thought it was Allan Jones.

They also had concerts on a Sunday evening in St. George's Hall in Stanbow Lane and it was always packed, because this was before cinemas were open on a Sunday. The programme ranged from Mary Mitchell, singing "Where E'er You Walk" and "Nymphs and Shepherds" to Terry West and "The Shrine of St. Cecelia" and Irene Blackamore dancing to "Oh! Salome", so there was something to please everyone's taste.

With their fathers and big brothers away from home the billeted airmen and soldiers were welcomed by the children. A surrogate relation came in handy for a variety of jobs: mending punctures, blowing up footballs, retrieving balls that had lodged in gutterings to name a few.

One airman, who was billeted with Mr. and Mrs. Fred Parker at the bottom of Edwin Street, proved his worth in a much more important way. The front of the houses face the river bank and fortunately he was looking out of a bedroom window, when he saw Frankie Welberry fall into the river. It was high tide and none of us could swim but he rushed out of the house, dived straight in and grabbed Frank, as he was going down for the third time.

Firing practise was carried out down the sea bank at the Kidstacks and at weekends and during the holidays one of our favourites trips was to ramble down the sea bank, bird-nesting as we went, and finish at the Kidstacks, where we would spend an hour or two looking for spent cartridges.

Trenches were dug in the Lord Nelson field for the recruits to practise warfare and we, of course, made full use of these to play out our own war games. They were in the shape of a Z and we chose sides, occupied the two main trenches then crept up on each other through the connecting trench or round the outsides. We bombarded each other with clods and someone always went home with a bloody nose.

The forces were not the only ones to practise with live ammunition; the Home Guard also used it for training. When I visit Wrangle churchyard I am reminded of the sad occasion, when a Home Guard unit was preparing for a possible invasion and a live hand-grenade exploded and killed Private Harness, whose grave is behind that of my wife's grandparents. Mr. Smith, who was the Station Master at Sibsey station and the unit Commander, also lost his arm in the accident.

Some of the lads, who had left school but were not yet eighteen, together with others, who had not passed the medical examination, travelled daily by bus to R.A.F. Coningsby, where they were employed building extra runways.   Mrs. Burton's son, Sid, was one of these and I used to watch for him coming home every evening.

I remember now how he used to step off the bus as it slowed down, never dreaming I would be doing the same sixteen years later, when he was the driver of the bus bringing me back from Wrangle, where I had been courting.

When the runways had been completed at Coningsby, several of the workers were flown to Iceland and spent the next four years building living quarters and new runways at airfields near Reykiavik.

BOROUGH OF BOSTON.

This is to certify that Mr. F.J.Mould

of 108 High Street Boston.

(National Registration Identity No. TGA047/1)

has been registered by the Corporation of Boston

for fire prevention duties.

Date 22.9.41

Initialled W.E.LL

Town Clerk.

An official fire watch card was necessary to enter buildings

17

ANY SPARE COUPONS?

Almost everything was rationed during the war but the shortage that affected children the most was, of course, sweets. The weekly ration was just 2 ozs., a small bar of chocolate or a bag of sweets.

Most parents gave their coupons to their children and a visit to grandparents or great aunts and uncles usually ended with a hopeful request for any spare coupons together with a charming smile. Shopkeepers could never sell any sweets without taking the coupons, as they could only buy from the wholesaler or manufacturer the amount they had coupons to cover. On the odd occasion, when a shop had sweets off the ration, maybe sticky boiled sweets from the bottom of a jar, a queue formed immediately, as if by magic.

The children from Staniland School supplemented their rations by buying licorice wood from Dickinson's shop. I do not know where it came from but I never knew anyone else to sell it and today anyone would be considered mad to ever put it in their mouths but in the prevailing conditions we were only too pleased to put a handful in our pockets; no need for a bag.

It looked like twigs off a tree but, when you started chewing, it turned yellow and tasted of licorice. Small boys were walking down the street resembling the old fishermen, chewing on their Pigtail twist.

Our parents were more preoccupied with the meat ration. Every family registered with a butcher and you could buy from no one else. Bob Creasey was our butcher and he did his utmost to satisfy his customers. We often enjoyed a rabbit pie, for rabbits were plentiful then and unrationed. Corned Beef was also a useful addition to your rations but in time it also became scarce.

In those days chickens were a luxury; most families only saw one at Christmas and turkeys were for the very rich. Uncle Ernie always brought us a large chicken for our

Christmas dinner and in return we gave him a Christmas cake. One good thing all chickens were free-range then; there were no battery hens until much later.

Country folk fared better: they were allowed to keep chickens but they had to have a licence to keep pigs, even if they just wanted to fatten one up for themselves.

Butter, margarine, lard and cooking fat were all rationed, together with eggs and again you had to register with a certain supplier. We did not sell groceries at that time; my grandmother ran the bakery shop and my mother had a cigarette and sweet shop next door.

We registered for butter and eggs with Ben Whyers, who had premises further along High Street, behind Scoxton's fruit and vegetable shop.

My parents had been friendly with Ben and his wife for many years, since they had all belonged to the Motor Cycle Club. My mother had little trouble persuading me to fetch the butter and eggs each week, as "Auntie Ivy", as we called her, had a parrot and, better still in the garden, a monkey.

Unrationed egg-powder was available and it was all right to make an omelette, when you had used all your eggs for that week but it was not much use for pancakes or Yorkshire puddings. Sugar, tea and cheese were also rationed but the weekly allowance satisfied most people and I can not remember any shortage of coffee but most families used liquid coffee essence, Camp, Red,White & Blue or Bev, as instant coffee had not then been introduced.

There was a separate book for clothing coupons and once again parents tended to sacrifice using them for themselves, as they needed them all for their growing children. An active black market developed with these, as older people without children often had enough clothes and they were willing to sell their coupons.

Petrol was rationed and the private motorist was restricted to journies of no more than ten miles. Many traders brought horses out of retirement to make their milk, bread or greengrocery deliveries. Our coal came by horse and cart and the horse knew the round better than the coalman. Drays, drawn by horses, brought the beer to the pubs sometimes from as far as Spalding.

C.& C. Wrights, the High Street ironmongers, used two horses to pull a cart, which made deliveries all over town under the guidance of Harry Dwyer. Harry was also landlord of the Robin Hood and he stabled the horses in the pub yard. The window at the back of the stable looked onto my grandfather's garden and he placed a garden bench below it, so I could watch the horses feeding.

Only fruit grown in this country was readily available; anything that came from overseas was difficult or impossible to buy. Bananas disappeared, until after the war and oranges were very scarce. Human nature dictates that, if something is unobtainable you desire it more than ever. People, who did not particularly like oranges before the war, found they were now craving them. If a shop was lucky enough to obtain a supply, regular and casual customers appeared from all over town and it was soon exhausted. The shopkeeper had to mark the back page of your ration book, whenever you managed to buy some oranges.

People spread their shopping among as many shops as possible, hoping to be considered as a regular customer at them all. Many items that were not rationed were still scarce and by necessity were kept under the counter, for the shopkeeper tried to avoid offending anyone by refusing them and then selling the same thing to a regular customer.

Tinned fruit and fish presented the worst problem, for the allocation was so small, that the grocer faced the impossible task of sharing maybe ten tins of peaches, pears or apricots among forty or fifty customers and fish was even worse; his allocation would probably be only five tins of salmon or crab.

Dried fruit was also a problem. Currants, sultanas or raisins were only available from the wholesalers three or four times a year and then it only worked out at about 8 ozs. per family. Most people put it by to make a cake or pudding for Christmas. If a wedding were planned, the mother of the bride had to rely on the mercy of her grocer and her neighbours to collect enough fruit for the bride's cake.

Cigarettes were in short supply and it was to be several years after the war, before things returned to normal. My job on a Monday evening was to help my mother share out the cigarettes we had received from Nicholsons, the wholesalers in Wide Bargate. We separated them into little piles under the counter and placed each customer's name on top. Most were allocated ten a day but some could not survive without twenty.

Woodbines and Park Drive were then the most popular brands and, even with supplies so limited, devotees of each were loathe to smoke any other brand. There were exceptions: Cyril Wright from the Goods Yard preferred Robins and Phil Smith, who worked on the dock, had Player's Weights. Towards the end of the war, when the position became even worse, smokers were obliged to buy any make they could find. That is when such brands as Turf and Nosegay appeared on the shelves.

The more affluent customers smoked Player's Navy Cut, Senior Service or Gold Flake, while the elite and those, who wished to make an impression, bought Piccadilly No. 1 or Churchmans but they were all scarce. Filter tips had not been invented but the few ladies, who smoked at that time, usually chose Du Maurier or Craven A, both of which sported cork tips.

Damage to the lungs was never considered then; in fact it was thought to be manly to smoke and advertisements proliferated. No self-respecting Hollywood hero would dream of making a film without being seen smoking and it was often an integral part of the story. Innumerable dying soldiers were given a cigarette, before they expired and no one will be allowed to forget the final scene in Now Voyager, where Paul Henreid lights two cigarettes and hands one to Bette Davis.

Carreras were the only company that were concerned with their smoker's health, for they advertised their cork-tipped Craven A as the cigarette that will not affect your throat.

It was when supplies were at their lowest that many smokers changed to rolling their own. Packet tobacco was never as scarce as cigarettes and the two popular brands they turned to were Franklyn's Mild and Ringers A1. Later these were supplanted by Golden Virginia and Harvest Gold.

I had a prized collection of cigarette packets and my early favourite was Black Cat, which disappeared soon after the war started. Other lads coveted my Passing Cloud and Three Castles packets, while one that created interest was a 20 Kensitas packet with an extra little compartment that had housed "four for your friends".

My favouritism had just been transferred to a packet that had contained 10 Joysticks and was twice as long as any other, when the Americans arrived and I was seduced by the glamorous Lucky Strikes, Phillip Morris, Chesterfields and Camels.

Most brands were sold in tens and twenties but Park Drive at one time could be bought in a packet containing fifteen and Woodbines were packed in fives but there was no lid to the pack, which resembled the packets used for sweet cigarettes. These fives helped, when we were sorting out the weekly piles: they were moved about towards the end of the week like pawns, especially if someone had been ill or on holiday, then their pile was divided between the others.

Mrs. Kate Fletcher was one of our most regular customers and she relied on us for twenty Woodbines every day. We always put them by in fives, as she came four times a day, maintaining that, if she took twenty in the morning, they would be gone by dinner time. She also enjoyed a quick chat with my mother and the walk up the lane gave her a short break from her chores.

On a Sunday we closed at lunchtime but she still relied on us to make her ration last the day, so she sometimes sent one of her grandchildren to the back door for her five Woodbines. This meant my mother going through the kitchen, then a short passage, then the living room into the shop. One Sunday Michael Fletcher ran the errand and it was raining, so he followed my mother through the kitchen but stopped in the passage. She came hurrying back from the shop, pushed open the door and sent him flying. There was a terrible thud followed by a loud wailing. We all ran to see what had happened, expecting his face to be bleeding or maybe a bump on his forehead but, when mother asked him where it hurt, he just repeated woefully through his sobs "Me bum! Me bum".

Staniland School Football team 1938/39

Back Row (left to right): Lesley Hull, Allen Molson, John Walker, Gerald Lee-dell, Stanley Rowett, A. Taylor, Walter Revell, Reg Wakefield. Front Row (left to right): "Cocker" Harvey, Eric Dennick, Mr. Wilson, Mr. Hudson (Headmaster), Lesley Oldland, Willy Lewis.

ON, STANILAND ON

The foundation stone for the original Staniland Board School was laid by the Chairman, Mr. R.W. Staniland on 18th. January, 1896.

The other members of the Board were: Mr. John Beaulah J.P. (Vice-Chairman), Mr. Joseph Clarke J.P. (Mayor), Mr. Joseph Cooke (Editor of Boston Guardian), Mr. Charles Newham Hunn, Father P.J. O'Donoghue (Catholic priest), and Rev. J. Stephenson M.A. (Vicar).

The Education Act setting up the Boards had been passed in 1871 but 25 years passed, before it was established in Boston and then in 1902 the Boards were abolished and education became the concern of the County Council.

Over the years Staniland school was always proud of both it's academic and sporting success. In pride of place on the wall in the Big Hall was the Honours Board, listing the names of all the children, who went on from Staniland to either the High School or the Grammar School. Mr. Hudson, the Headmaster throughiout the war, indeed until 1952, was meticulous in adding pupils' names, as soon as their success was confirmed.

I had just started at the Infants, when war was declared, and my teacher was Miss Darby, followed by Miss Kent and the Headmistress was Miss Luesley. I do not remember much of those first two years but once I had progressed to the Big School I encountered Miss Parker and no one forgets that experience.

Ruby Parker, later became Mrs. Meadows and she taught at Staniland for many years. In retrospect I realise she was a marvellous teacher, laying a solid foundation for others to build on over the following years. At the time fear was my principal feeling and it extended out of the classroom. I used to walk home up Fydell Crescent and along High Street and the top half of Fydell Crescent at that time was exclusively woodyards. Cars were parked at intervals at the side of the woodyards and Geoff Mitcham and myself were intrigued by the noise made by wind escaping from car tyres. I realise now how stupid a thing it was to do but neither of us gave any thought to the consequences of our prank, until we suddenly realised we were being watched.

Miss Parker had approached behind us and I still remember the feeling of utter dread, when I turned and saw her face. The use drained out of my legs and I could not move and that night was one of the longest of my life, knowing that we were to be cained by Mr. Hudson the next morning. It was the only time I was ever cained and I remember little of the actual punishment but I shall always remember her face.

My second year was entrusted to Mrs. Akehurst, who had previously been Miss Avery. Mr. Akehurst had also taught at Staniland, until joining the forces. She made learning interesting and whetted our appetites for further knowledge. The honing was left to Mrs. Mauveley in the third year, the scholarship class. She was kindness personified but she kept perfect control of her class and most of the credit for any successes in the examinations was attributed rightfully to her.

One popular teacher, who never actually taught me, was Miss Calthrop but, while I was a pupil, she left the school and the occasion is printed indelibly on my memory. The popularity of Staniland made it necessary to find an extra classroom and this was accomplished by using a room behind St. James's Church. It was divided by a curtain and two classes crossed over George Street every day. However on the day Miss Calthrop left the whole school crossed over into the Church itself to say goodbye to one of the most loved and respected teachers, that ever taught.

We were breaking up for the Christmas holidays and she stood in front of the assembly and sang "In the Bleak Mid-winter" and, as we came out of church, the girls were crying openly and the boys were trying to stifle their tears.

One day, while I was in Miss Parker's class, I witnessed one of the most memorable fires in Boston's history. Ronnie Heughs, who more recently has featured in the local press for running a model railway, giving children rides at such venues as the Carrington Traction Engine Rally, was inches taller than the rest of the class, so Miss Parker always placed him on the back row to prevent anyone hiding behind him. He noticed smoke and flames rising from the top of Bedford's mill, which was directly opposite our classroom.

He told Miss Parker and she telephoned the Fire Brigade from Mr. Hudson's office but they had already arrived, when she returned to her room. She never attempted to return to the tables we were learning but let us watch from the windows. There was no question of evacuating the school, for the mill stood back on the other side of Fydell Crescent and it was probably decided that we were in the best place and out of harm's way.

We noted and admired the orderly but hurried actions of the firemen, who took full advantage of the water stored in a sunken bricked pit at the side of the mill. They eventually brought the fire under control and order was restored in the classroom but we were all too excited to learn much that day.

Two weeks before the Christmas holidays each year pillar boxes were stood in the classroom and we posted cards in it to our friends in the class. The teacher opened it on the last day of term and we walked up for our cards, as our names were called out. The prettiest girl and the most popular boy were kept busy that day.

Soon after the war started one or two new faces appeared at school and fresh accents were heard. Children from London and one or two from Hull were evacuated, when the air raids became too regular and prolonged. We only had one evacuee in our class, Arthur Hollamby, and his brother Raymond was in my brother's class. By Christmas he was popular with the girls, because of his curly hair, and with the boys, because of his prowess on the football field, so he received more than his share of cards.

I came to know him quite well later in life. When he came home out of the forces, he brought back to Boston a beautiful wife, Inge, a German girl. They spent their early married years in a flat at the home of his best friend, Geoff Drummond, who lived for a time opposite our shop in High Street.

Exercise books, pencils, ink and pen nibs were all in short supply during the war and we were taught to economise and never to waste anything. One thing, however, that was never scarce at Staniland school was india rubbers. When the Regal cinema was built in 1938, the top surface of the floor in the foyer was made of rubber and the off-cuts and all unused pieces were kindly given to the school by Mr. Howden.

The school motto was "On, Staniland On" and Mr. Hudson, the Headmaster, had a banner, on which the words were emblazoned and he displayed it as he patrolled the touchline at all important school football matches. His enthusiasm was matched by Mr. Burton, his counterpart at Carlton Road School and the two had several encounters, because most of the finals were fought out between Staniland and Carlton Road with an occasional appearance by Park Board.

The other teams in the School League were St. Botolphs, Tower Road, St. Nicholas, Shodfriars, St. Thomas's and Kirton.

All the matches were played on the pitch in the Lord Nelson field and I remember Staniland winning the league in two consecutive seasons, while George "Bunty" Stow played in goal. He allowed few shots to go past him but the whole team were well above average and they played the game as it should be played today. No time was wasted playing across the pitch; the full backs and centre half cleared their lines; the half backs and inside forwards moved the ball up the field and out to the wingers, "Bowie" Barton and "Whippet" Bray, and they centred for the centre forward, "Wokka" Revell to hit it or head in into the net. Others in the team were "Cocker" Harvey, Reg Wakefield and Maurice Dobbs.

Margaret Maddrell, who moved to Staniland in 1942, was walking home from St. Thomas's School to Ransome Place along the river bank in London Road, when she saw what looked like German soldiers pacing up and down the Swing Bridge. She was only seven at the time but, knowing the war was on, she thought we had been invaded and ran back quickly to school. Others had done the same but their fears were laid to rest, when they were reassured that it was a film crew making "One Of Our Aircraft Is Missing", telling how the airmen from a crashed bomber in Holland return home, helped by the Dutch Resistance.

Michael Powell and Emeric Pressburger were the directors and the six members of the bomber crew were played by Godfrey Tearle, Eric Portman, Hugh Williams, Bernard Miles, Hugh Burden and Emrys Jones. Googie Withers, Pamela Brown and Joyce Redman were three members of the Resistance, who helped then to escape and Robert Helpman, the famous ballet dancer was a German officer.

The film also marked the acting debut of Peter Ustinov and probably helped him to decide to make a career of acting in and directing films. It was also the debut of Jimmy Baker but his name did not appear on the credits, when it was shown later at the Regal.

A group of us were watching one day, when they were shooting a scene, where the airmen were climbing out of a window down a rope. One of the houses near Midgeley's shop down Skirbeck Quarter had a round window, which served the purpose ideally. A member of the film crew came over and stood appraising us for a while, then asked Jimmy, who lived in Oxford Street, if he would like to be in the film.

He had to turn up a few days later and they dressed him in suitable clothes and clogs; told him what they wanted him to do and he spent the day filming. In the finished film he is on screen for about ten seconds, running across a cobbled courtyard to take a message to the airmen, when some Germans stop him but one kicks his behind and they all laugh but the message is delivered.

Jimmy enjoyed his brief encounter with fame and for years afterwards he was teased about being a film star.

The climax of the film, when the airmen were making their bid for freedom in a rowing boat, featured the Swing Bridge prominently and they must have been shooting these scenes, when Margaret Maddrell was frightened.
At the time Margaret lived within a stone's throw of the Swing Bridge in Ransome Place, which was also known as California Place. Her house backed onto the coalyard and the railway line, on which the trains went to the dock over the bridge, then returned to the coalyard. She was playing outside one day, when a German plane dived down and machine-gunned a train but a neighbour hearing the loud whining sound overhead grabbed her and took her indoors, under the stairs. When they saw the bullet holes all around the houses, she realised how lucky she had been.

She moved down Station Street the next year and lived next door to the Great Northern pub, directly opposite my grandmother and that is when she came to Staniland School. She joined my class and the other girls were: Barbara Blackwell, Merany Craven, Elaine Davy, Alma Dowse, Sylvia Fox, Mauveline Gillings, Beryl Goodman, Pamela Kinsey, Margaret Lacy, Pat Ladds, Barbara Maddison, Janet Midgelow, Doreen Read, Thelma Reed, Marjorie Revell, Mary Robinson, Violet Simpson, Janet

Troops, the twins, Eileen and Marlene Watts, Cynthia Wright, Pauline Blackamore and Maureen Hall. My apologies if I have missed anyone.

For some reason I find it harder to remember the boys: Barry Barton, Peter Blackamore, Brian Blackburn, Jimmy Brewster, Gordon Butcher, Alan Chester, Peter Day, Victor Emery, Norman Forbes, Basil Gardner, Philip Green, Noel Holgate, Arthur Hollamby, Derek Holland, Brian Jackson, Neal Lockwood, Peter Luff, Bob Marriott, Alastair Massingham, Geoff Mitcham,   Denis Robins, Horace Simpson, Ron Southwell, Derek Thompson and Ronny Thompson.

I was ten years old in 1944 and I had taken the examinations to go to the Grammar School but my name was not included in the list of scholarships and free places, so I was resigned to returning to Staniland for another year, as I had a further chance the next year.

Towards the end of August my parents received a letter to say I had beed awarded a Parry scholarship and I would be starting at the Grammar School in September. After the initial panic, my mother organised my uniform and the minor paraphernalia and, when the day came, I was standing near the wall in the Grammar School playground with the other new boys, fully equipped.

We never found out if I had done well or if I had been next on the list and lucky to be chosen for a scholarship that was only given occasionally from money, left for that purpose by the Thomas Parry Trust in 1875. We thought it might provide a clue, if I were placed in the A form but we were still no wiser, because I was placed in 3A2. I was always grateful for this afterwards, because the boys in 3A1 took Latin and we took German. 1944 was the last year that parents could pay for their children to go to Grammar School and they changed the system of numbering classes the next year. Whereas previously forms 1 and 2 had been exclusively for boys, whose parents had paid for them to start at eight or nine, now everyone started in form 1.

In 1945 ten of us from 3A2 were placed in 2A and, when the rest of the class had Latin periods, we had to change classrooms and join the German period.

One repercussion of my sudden departure from Staniland was the change in attitude of my former friends. Like most boys of that age I belonged to a gang and we had strict rules. We had recently expelled Roy "Inky" Barton from the gang and his only crime was that he had flitted from Pulvertoft Lane to Cheyney Street. We had all signed a typewritten letter telling him of our decision.

So my fate was sealed as soon as they knew I was going to be a "Grammar School puppy dog". It all sounds unimportant now but at the time it was deadly serious to a ten-year old and it caused me a few sleepless nights. The gang consisted of Jacky Tebbs, Bob Marriott, Barry Barton and Ronny Thompson and we used to meet on the river bank near Gostelow's slip. For the uninitiated a slip is an inlet in the bank, strengthened by rocks, where a fishing smack could be secured, while it was being repaired or creasoted.

We knew how all the passages in Pulvertoft Lane and Edwin Street interlinked and played endless games of being secret agents chased by the enemy and trying to return to our headquarters. There was no danger involved, unless we became too noisy, then we needed all our wits to dodge the inevitable bowl of water from Mrs. Woods.

All this excitement was now denied me but my time was soon filled by a new experience....homework.

CAN I DO YOU NOW SIR?

Only a few families close to London had television sets, when the war started but everyone had a radio. Most of these needed accumulators and a regular job was to take one accumulator to Allens to be charged and bring the fully-charged one back. As with television today, we all had our favourite programmes and knew which could be heard each night.

Itma with all it's characters and catch-phrases is always the first to be remembered but there were many more: Hi Gang, Happidrome, Much Binding In The Marsh, The Charley Chester Show, Variety Bandbox and, of course, Workers' Playtime with Bill Gates, which travelled around the country and broadcast variety shows from factories and munition works nearly every dinner time.

Every act had a catch-phrase: Nat Mills and Bobby "We can't both speak at once, can we?"; Horace Kenny with his "Merry, rollicking, laughing fireman's song"; Harry Hemsley "What did Horace say?"; Bill Kerr. the man from Wogga Wogga "I've only got four minutes". He must have been young, for he still acts in Australian films today.

Every singer had a peculiar introduction: Cavan O'Conner, the strolling vagabond; Arthur Tracy, the street singer or the opening bars of their signature tune told you who was coming on: "Hear my song Violetta" heralded Josef Locke; "My heart and I" introduced Richard Tauber.

Tommy Handley's Itma was the one programme no one missed; you heard the many catch-phrases, wherever you went: Mrs. Mopp "Can I do you now sir", Ali Oop "I go...I cum back", Colonel Chinstrap "I don't mind if I do sir", then there was "After you Claude..No, after you Cecil", "This is Funf speaking" and many more.

Hi GANG! was nearly as popular. It starred Bebe Daniels and Ben Lyon, together with Vic Oliver, who was married to Winston Churchill's daughter. Each week they pulled Ben Lyon's leg about appearing with Jean Harlow in

"Hell's Angels" in 1930.

Richard Murdoch split from Arthur Askey to start Much Binding in the Marsh with Kenneth Horne, Sam Costa and Maurice Denham and it was popular for many years after the war. It was my father's favourite programme, until Take It From Here started.

Happidrome had a famous opening song: "We three from Happidrome, working for the B.B.C.; Ramsbottom and Enoch and Me". Frank Randall was Ramsbottom, Robbie Vincent was Enoch and Harry Norris was Mr. Lovejoy. Everytime Enoch came on Mr. Lovejoy would greet him with some derogatory remark, such as: "Here he comes, a pennyworth of chips, looking for his vinegar" and Enoch would say "Let me tell you, I've got blue blood in my veins".

The Charley Chester show started towards the end of the war and all the boys started talking about Whippet Quick and came to school quoting couplets like: "Living in the jungle, living in a tent. Better than a prefab, no rent."

I must admit I never listened to his show but he was very popular and was still on the radio a few years ago.

Variety Bandbox was the highlight of every Sunday evening. The hour-long show always finished with a top comedian: for years Frankie Howerd alternated with Derek Royle. Frankie went on to be really famous but Derek Royle, whom I preferred, lost favour and few remember him now. Over the years the B.B.C. have made a habit of building people up, then dropping them, when at their peak, like Kathy Kirby, Dave King and Grace Kennedy.

Michael Howard occasionally topped the bill on Variety Bandbox: his speciallity was the shaggy dog story, used later by Les Dawson, where he spends two minutes developing a joke, then the ending is an anti-climax. For example, he told once of the man, who received a present from a distant relative and it arrived in a crate, labelled "The last Rari in the world.

He looked it up in an encyclopaedia and found it was a pre-historic animal, that could still be found living in the Himalayas. Michael Howard would then explain the man's difficulties in feeding it and keeping it safe, before eventually saying that he had to finally destroy it. The problem then was how to kill it? He tried shooting it but it's hide was too tough; he tried to poison it but the poison had no effect; he tried to drown it but it was a strong swimmer; then he had an idea; he took it to the highest cliff he could find, placed it on the edge and with the help of ten friends prepared to push it over.

At this point the animal turned round and, speaking for the first time, said "It's a long way to tip a Rari."

Other comedians, who came to the fore on Variety Bandbox were Leon "Shakespeare" Cortez, who once came to the Odeon; he modernised Shakespeare and finished his act with "Hi hi, that's your lot: Reg Dixon, "I'm proper poorly" and Arthur English, the wide boy with a kipper tie, "Open the cage, play the music."

Music Hall on a Saturday night was the other weekly variety show and I remember one Saturday night near the end of the war, when Max Wall was the final act with his typical short jokes: "My lord, there is a lady without". "Without what?" "Without food and clothing." "Then feed her and show her in." The show always opened with a new comedian and this week they introduced a young lad, who as always was going to go far but this one did, Max Bygraves.

The value of the cinema to the morale of the country was recognised and in 1942 for the first time cinemas were allowed to open on Sundays. It proved to be very popular and the queues started at 6 o'clock, although the progamme commenced at 7 o'clock.

Two films were always shown and usually they had been shown during the week three or four years previously, long enough for most people to have forgotten the ending. I was at the Odeon that first Sunday and the main film was "The Rat" with Anton Walbrook and Rene Ray, followed the second week by Gordon Harker and Alastair Sim in "Inspector Hornleigh". Both these films were originally released in 1938.

My first excursions to see a film were not to a cinema but to a small room above the vestry at St. James's Church in George Street. The Rev. Johnny Jordan gave film shows for children on a Saturday afternoon. He was both the M.C. and the projectionist and he played records on a gramophone before and after the show. Today, if I hear Glenn Miller's recording of "Elmer's Tune", I can imagine myself back in that room in 1940.

Two years later I was considered old enough to go to the Mickey Mouse Club at the Odeon on a Saturday morning. "Every Saturday morning where do we go? Getting into mischief? Oh dear no! To the Mickey Mouse Club with our badges on. Every Saturday morning at the O DE ON.

The Regal also had their Hoodoo Club but my sister and brother had always gone to the Odeon, so I followed suit. The programme never varied; after we had all sung the club song, there would be a cartoon, then an episode of the current serial, maybe Flash Gordon or The Three Mesketeers and finally the main film, either a western, a spy film or a jungle adventure.

I soon transferred my allegiance from the Mickey Mouse Club to whichever cinema was showing the best film that week and I progressed from Saturday morning to Saturday afternoon. Our lives were shaped temporarily to a great extent by the film we saw that particular week.

If it was Errol Flynn in "The Adventures of Robin Hood", the trees down the Polypads were stripped and we all had bows and quivers full of arrows on our backs. When Tyrone Power was in "The Mark of Zorro", we all sported plasters on our knuckles, through our amateur attempts at sword-fighting and all the sheds and coal-house doors were suddenly decorated with huge Zs.

The Nelson field was the scene of battle, after we had watched Robert Taylor in "Bataan" or Brian Donlevy in "Wake Island". The trenches became wider, as we dug lumps out of them to represent hand grenades and we defended the concrete pillbox to the last man.

About this time also I was introduced to film comedians. Janet Stephens, who helped my mother in the shop agreed to take me one evening to see George Formby in "Much Too Shy" at the Regal. Later she met and married Charley Drury, who played at one time for Boston United, but at the time she did not object to the company of a well-behaved lad.

I determined there and then never to miss a George Formby film and I soon widened my interest to include Will Hay, Max Miller, Frank Randall and, of course, Old Mother Riley. I already knew that Phyllis Vickers from the fish and chip shop was Arthur Lucan's niece and that his proper name was Towle, because his brother Tom Towle was a customer in our shop. I was really excited, however, when Pete Motley took my brother and I to buy some rabbits off Mrs. Ladds down Rowell Row and she told us she was Old Mother Riley's sister.

IS IT ONE OF OURS?

Compared with some other towns and cities Boston did not suffer from too many air-raids during the war. In the first two years the German bombers headed for the industrial areas and in the latter stages, after they had lost most of their planes, the flying bombs were set to explode further inland; they did not want to waste them by possibly falling into the North Sea.

The sirens were sounded regularly, however, as their bombers, often passed over on the way to their target. Our fighter planes tried to meet them, before they reached their objective, so they also flew over this area and, of course, our own bombers flew mainly from Lincolnshire and Norfolk. At first few people could tell one plane from another and every five minutes someone would pop out of a shelter to ask a warden "Is it one of ours?

Eventually we learned to distinguish between a fighter and a bomber; the fighter obviously passed over more quickly and the drone of the bomber lasted much longer. It was more difficult to tell from the sound, if it were a German plane but the fire-watchers became experts. They were all issued with charts giving front and side views of all planes but on a dark night they had to rely on the sound of the engines.

Each area of the town had it's own fire-watching section. My father was in charge of the High Street watch and I still have the rosta book he used. Four men were on duty each night and they split into two pairs: one pair took up position on the flat roof of a house near the top of Oxford Street and I belief the other pair were stationed on Brough's roof at the northern end of High Street.

Their main job was to watch out for incendiary bombs and inform the Fire Service.

Boston's air raid wardens were split into ten areas, under the overall command of Chief Warden H.E. Jasper Sharpe of Jesmond House, Witham Bank.

The railway station area's Head Warden was Mr. F.L. Oldham and the wardens were: J.E. Allett, V. Atkinson, S. Baldock, J. Best, C.C. Compton, W. Goodrum, W.A. Gore, F.K. Howes, F. Julian, W.C. Langstaff, A. Meads, N.Newton, H.L. Norris, F. Odling, S.W. Polkinghorne, T.E. Riley, S.C. Smith, H.R. Taylor, F. Trevor, G.W. Turner, J. Turner, H. Turpin and E. Walmsley.

The Central Park area's Head Warden was Mr. H.W. Crampton and the wardens were: H.A. McDowell, F. Morley, T. Crick, J.S. Sargeant, G. Broadley, G. Brocklesby, N.C. Chaplin, W. Ryan, J.G. Coupland, H, Bringeman, W. Tippet, A. Everett, R.J. Kitchen, L. Hackford, J.H. Tebbutt, R. Holland, A,H, Peatling, A.W. Haynes, R.A.M. Wright, and S.J. Williamson.

The Main Ridge area's Head Warden was Mr. Phil Rysdale and the wardens were: A.E. Appleby, G.E. Ashberry, J. Chester, A. Coleman, H. Comer, A. Dawson, H.H. Holmes, P.R. Keal, Mrs. F. Leary, A.P. Loveley, W. Mableson, G. Meades, J.F. Norman, E.H. Page, G.H. Panton, W.H. Pawley, W.H. Pears, C.W. Peberdy, A. Storr, W.A. Sutton, R.S. Tooley and C.E. White.

The Fydell Crescent area's Head Warden was Mr. J.R. Stanwell and the wardens were: R.S. Appleby, E.W. Barrand, J.W. Bell, J.B. Brightwell, F.R. Caress, G.W. Clarke, L.A. Clarke, C.W. Coaten, T.H. Cooley, R. Creasey, A. Johnson, R.Mackman, K.J. Palmer, F. Parker, H.E. Pulford, G.W. Richardson, W.H. Scuffham, A.E. Staples, H. Stead, S.D. Trigg, G. Twiddy, J. Waddingham, E. Ward, K. Welberry and E. Wright.

The Skirbeck Road area's Head Warden was Capt. H.H. Morris and the wardens were: W.E. Adcock, C.G. Atkin, D.G. Borrill, Miss M. Brocklesby, G. Cutland, F.P. Egerton, W.A.G. Flack, G.B. Gibson, A.T. Hayes, S. Hayes, Mrs. L. Jessop, W.M. Jessop, T. Kirtley, K. Lancaster, A. Lunn, Mrs. J.M. Lunn, S.E. Lane, Mrs. E.M. Morris, J.W.B. Newton, W.H. Potter, R.C. Scott, F. Borrill, A Lawther, A. Christie and Dr. J.B. Jackson.

The Ingelow Avenue area's Head Warden was Mr. J.W. Addlesee and the wardens were: E.H. Allison, M. Baker, G. Broughton, J.A. Cheshire, G. Craven, W. Dawkes, W. Farram, K.C. Frost, G. Green, R. Hammerton, G. Hooper, W. Jeffrey, J. McKenny, P. Smith, A. Taylor, Mrs. N.D. Nussey, A. Reeson, G.S. Muir, J.B. Richardson, J.J. Leedell, Miss N. Parker, A. Wander, J.T. Waterstone and N.B. Royal. The Horncastle Road area's Head Warden was Mr. C.W. Rogers and the wardens were: D.R.K. Bond, A.H. Chester, Mrs. M. Cockrill, E.J. Dawson, R.H. Elliss, L. Holland, Mrs. F.E. Lunn, R.A. Lunn, W.B. Land, W. Kent, D.F. Shepherd, W.P. Stow, E.F. Sykes, A. Taylor, A. Wattam, J. Tooley, Miss M.A. Whelbourn and F. Morley.

The Tower Road area's Head Warden was Mr. T.H. Rickard and the wardens were: H.G. Ackrill, Mrs. Arch, S.N. Addy, J.W. Allen, H. Baker, J.E. Baumber, G.W. Boothby, S.F. Cammack, A.C. Burton, S. Beakey, W.H. Christian, C. Clayton, B. Cooper, A.R. Davies, T.B. Dawson, J.W. Dawson, F. Day, H. Evison, H.G. Frost, J.W. Gledhill, J.W. Harrison, H. Langstaff, J.W. Lockwood, A.P. Jackson, C.F. Johnson, H. Futter, N.H. Middlebrook, T.M. Moffatt, S. Morril, R. Ostler, M.M. Parkinson, R. Peck, W.H. Rutt, J.L. Semper, H.C. Senior, C. Sinclair, G.J. Stead, F.R. White, Mrs. F.R. White and T.R. Wing.

The Sleaford Road area's Head Warden was Mr. W. Hamer and the wardens were: W.L. Alexander, W.E. Anderson, D.O. Browning, H. Damms, G. Davis, E. Dickens, I.T, Fraser, S.B. Hampshire, W.H. Harrison, C.E. King, A.L.Maddison, W. Massie, B.D. Parker, S. Parkin, H.T. Read, T.D.C. Rosser, A.B. Stephenson, R. Tryner, J. Walker, C.F. Wilkinson and W.H. Wilson.

The St. Thomas's Church area's Head Warden was Mr. A. Walker and the wardens were: E.D. Bagot, Mrs. M.K. Bagot, L. Baines, B.J. Buck, S. Cooper, G.W. Dell, H.M. Dickson, T.M. Chalmers, W.S. Dawson, G.H. Gilchrist, Mrs. G.H. Gilchrist, Mrs. G. Grigor, Mrs. E. Ingamells, P.W. Kitchen, R. Sharper, C. Valentine, Mrs. M.E. Walker, J. Watts,

R.C. Pryor, J. Grigor snr., J. Grigor jnr. and C. Wain.

There were two first aid posts at Allan House in Carlton Road and at Bargate. Dr. A. Eckford and Dr. S.S. Rendall with Mr. J.C. Laight L.D.S. as anesthetist were at Allan House and Dr. R.C. Flower and Dr. G.R. Usmar with Mr. D. MacTaggart L.D.S. as anesthetist were at Bargate. In addition there were six first aid posts at Stinson's Garage, Municipal Buildings, Fenside Road, Mill Inn, Spilsby Road, Unicorn Inn, Tattershall Road and Boston Dock

There was also a County Council mobile first aid unit stationed in Boston. It was actually a converted furniture van with a large amount of medical stores and equipment. If a major incident had occured at some part of the town some distance from the fixed posts, this mobile unit would have proceeded to the site and rendered immediate medical aid to the injured. Dr. A.C. Gee and Dr. M.J. Sheehan with anesthetists Paul Moran and Mr. Williams were attached to this unit.

There were six detachments of the British Red Cross Society covering Boston under the following Commandants: Mrs. Vernon Clark, Miss F.S. Isaac, Miss M. Hildred, Mrs. L. Giles, Mrs. R. Clifton and Miss S. Groom. Dr. Fielding was the local Ambulance A.R.P. Officer.

During the war the Central Fire Station was in West Street and there were sub-stations in Bargate and Skirbeck. The Chief Officer was F.F. Carter and the Second Officer was H.W. Goodliff. The engineers were W.H. Pestell and G. Jessup and there were only eight other full-time firemen. However there were no less than a hundred and ten men in the Auxiliary Fire Brigade under Divisional Officer C. Crick.

The Borough Engineer, Mr. D.G. Cockrill and Assistant Engineer, Mr. C.R. Theobald were in charge of three rescue parties, each with their own lorry, two decontamination squads and two road and sewer squads, all on stand-by in case of emergencies.

The rescue squads, apart from helping people out of bombed buildings, were also responsible for making the buildings safe, even if it involved demolition.

Many of these personnel would have been called out early one Monday morning in 1941, when a bomb fell at the top of Liquorpond Street. A German bomber must have been returning home without dropping it's last bomb and it was probably aimed at the Dock.

Previously the only bombs dropped on Boston had been incendiaries and had caused little damage, so people were caught off their guard and few were in the shelters. We were sleeping downstairs on camp beds and the explosion dumped us on the floor and brought soot down the chimney all over us. My father was in the bakehouse and my mother was just opening the shop, so it must have been around 6.30 a.m. It is a sobering thought to realise, if that bomb had dropped two seconds later, it would possibly have hit our house.

As it was the passage running parallel to Liquorpond Street, which opened on to High Street at the side of Brown's grocery shop, was demolished and damage was caused to many houses in the vicinity, chimney stacks were dislodged, fully or partly, halfway down Liquorpond Street and windows were blown in. A young apprentice baker was just arriving to work at Fox's bakehouse, next door to White's fish and chip shop in High Street and, when my mother looked out of our shop window, his shirt was white at the front but, when he turned round, it was red: a piece of shrapnel had pierced his back.

One of the wardens, who had been on duty, was missing: Mr. Pulford actually lodged with a lady in High Street and he had popped home to the toilet. As with many houses at the time, the toilet was outside and the bomb fell within one hundred yards of him. The door flew off, hit him on the head and he was concussed. When they eventually found him, he was still sat on the toilet.

Many people were injured but the only person to be killed was Mrs. Gee, whose granddaughter, Maureen Hall, was in my class.   Maureen sometimes spent the night with her grandmother but fortunately she was not there when the bomb fell.

For weeks afterwards, as we walked to school down Liquorpond Street, the smell of soot persisted and workmen were busy repairing the bomb damage.

At 2.30 a.m. on a morning in June, 1941 Jim Walker, who now lives in Wickford, Essex, was in Tower Street, calling up a driver for early duty, when he saw a German bomber flying very low.   He actually heard the whistling noise of a bomb coming down, then an almighty explosion and he just had time to put on his tin helmut, when a brick hit him on the head and knocked him down.   He picked himself up and tried to go up James street but the smoke and soot prevented him.

The bomb had fallen on a row of houses at the top of James Street and killed several people.   There was extensive damage to the Royal George and to Loveley's bakehouse.   Ken, Ray, Peter and their parents slept in the front but the two daughters, Kathleen and Audrey slept in a bedroom over the bakehouse and they were both killed.

In one of the houses Mrs. Harris lived with her three children and they were all looking forward to their father coming home on leave.   They had just flitted from Edwin Street and he was coming to see their new home but they were all killed and their home obliterated.

Rescue Party No. 2 was soon on the scene and they helped the survivors to safety, then recovered the bodies, before making the area safe.   The bodies were taken down James Street to the Great Northern public house and placed in the backyard.   Margaret Maddrell, who had moved from Ransom Place to 21, Station Street, next door to the Great Northern, remembers looking out of her bedroom window and seeing the bodies laid there, until they could be taken away for identification.

The bomb was probably intentioned for the Railway Station but again the aim proved faulty.

In another raid a bomb fell in Main Ridge on houses, where the Post Office Sorting Yard now stands. I am not sure when this occured but Mr. R.H. Stephens remembers his father-in-law, Sydney Emery, who was a member of Rescue Party No. 2, was also involved in recovering the body of a lady, who was killed in that raid.

Another bomb fell on Holland Brothers at the junction of Wide Bargate and Tawney Street, where Iceland now have a store, but fortunately this one did not explode. Two wardens, Mark Parkinson and Austin Davies, arrived on the scene and papers from Holland's office were floating down and they could see a crater. Austin was about to step forward, when Mark shouted to warn him he was standing near a bomb. The area was cordoned off and people were told to stay clear, until the Bomb Disposal Squad rendered it harmless.

Towards the end of the war raids became less frequent and once again some people found it too much trouble to go to the shelters, especially if it entailed leaving their beds. By 1944 we had moved to 65, High Street, a large house next door to the Royal Oak public house. It had been at one time a nurses' home and had railings along it's front and up the steps that led to the front door. These had disappeared as soon as the war started and the house had been divided into two separate dwellings. The part next door to Fred Herring's cobblers shop was the home of Mr. and Mrs. Hatfield.

We still used the shelter at the top of Pulvertoft Lane, as we knew everyone there and conversation was easy but the distance involved was too far for my brother and mother reluctantly left him in bed, when the siren sounded during the night. One night he was alone in the house and a German plane started flying low over the town firing indiscriminately.

We could hear plainly from inside the shelter, for it transpired that it was not a machine gun he was firing but cannon shells. When my father popped over from the bakehouse, mother insisted that he fetched my brother to the shelter.

He waited while all seemed quiet, then hurried along High Street and persuaded my brother to return with him but, as soon as they left the house, the plane returned. The pilot must have been pleased to have found a moving target and he swooped down firing at them. They threw themselves flat on the ground and waited a while, before running back to the refuge of the shelter.

We were not sure, if we should believe their story but the next morning they were vindicated, when we saw the holes in the wall of the house opposite, where the cannon shells had hit at about head height. There was an opening, where the Post Office Telephone maintenance vans used to emerge early every morning, and the house always had a painted advertisement on the wall. That morning there were two holes straight through a tin of Ideal milk.

The Air Raid Wardens of Area No.4 (Fydell crescent area) taken on VE Day, May 8th 1945
Back Row (left to right): Larry Clarke, Mr. E. Ward, Mr. Barton, Arthur Atkin, George Twiddy, Harry Welberry.
Middle Row (left to right): Mr. G. Clarke, -----, -----, -----, Bill Scuffham, Fred Parker, -----, -----.
Front Row (left to right): Jack Brightwell, Alf Staples, Mr. H. Pulford, Mr. E. Wright.

LEAVE YOUR DOORS AND WINDOWS OPEN

Several planes came down in the Wash or on the banks of the four rivers that join in the Wash. An Air Sea Rescue unit was stationed at the Marine Hotel at Freiston Shore for just such an emergency.

One night, after the United States had entered the war, one of their planes crashed in the Wash and the Air Sea Rescue unit was called out but, when they found the plane, all the crew were dead.

There must have been some innovative equipment on board the plane, for eight American Air Force technicians arrived immediately and went out to the crashed plane every day, until they had recovered all the instruments and personal belongings of the dead airmen.

They lodged at the Marine and Ethel and Austin Davies remembered the time they were there as one of the busiest but most interesting periods of their tenancy.

In some of the large bombing raids towards the end of the war planes from several different airfields assembled in the sky over this area, before making a combined assault on Germany.

At 5.30 a.m. on 13th. July, 1944 a Liberator took off from R.A.F. Marham in Norfolk to take part in a raid on Saarbrucken. The weather was poor with rain and heavy overcast conditions.

There were nine in the crew. The pilot was N.J. Hunt, the co-pilot was P.R. Roetzel, the bomber was W.J. Hession, the engineer W.L. McKinzie, the radio operator was H.C. Wilkinson, the nose gunner was W.E. Caurington, the right waist-gunner was M. Osment, the left-waist gunner was D.L. McEwan and the tail gunner was L.A. Jackson.

Although it was summer, soon after take-off ice formed on the wings but it was soon cleared and by 6-00 a.m. they joined planes from other airfields, assembling over Eastville and Wrangle.   At this point the ice re-appeared but worse this time and, in spite of Captain Norman Hunt's efforts, the engines failed and the aircraft went out of control.

These details were given later by the sole survivor, the left-waist gunner, D.L. McEwan, who attempted to leave the plane through the waist window but was trapped half in and half out.   He was made semi-conscious, when he hit his head on the side of the aircraft, but was luckily thrown clear and managed to pull his ripcord, before losing consciousness.

By now it was 6.30 a.m. and he came round about 8.00 a.m. with three children looking concerned, standing over him.   The children were Bernard Codd and his sisters, Ena and Barbara.   They had been woken by the crash at 6.30 a.m. and saw from their bedroom window that it had happened just along the road from their farmhouse.

They went to see if anyone needed help but had to return home, when the ammunition in the plane started exploding.   As they neared home, they noticed a parachute in their father's field.   They ran over and found D.L. McEwan semi-conscious and asking for a U.S. medic.

One of them ran home and raised the alarm and a Home Guard patrol arrived but they were frightened to move him, because his legs were folded under him and they feared he had broken his back.

However, when Doctor Bee arrived, he was pleased to tell him he was just badly bruised and shaken.   He learned later that all his mates had been killed.

The plane had crashed on an uncultivated piece of land at Wrangle Lowgrounds near the Black Bull.   The land is now used for allotments.   The tail fell off two miles nearer to the sea and wreckage was scattered over a large area. The body of the plane had made a hole 50 feet by 30 feet and thrown up a bank of earth six feet high.

Mr. Joseph Johnson, the Headmaster of Wrangle Common school, lived in the schoolhouse, only three hundred yards away from the crash. He was Deputy Head Warden for the village and had a telephone upstairs near his bed, so he rang Control immediately and all the local roads were closed. The Boston Fire Brigade arrived within twenty minutes and a R.A.F. fire tender soon afterwards with foam extinguishers.

The fireman were warned not to go too close, because of the ammunition going off and the immediate neighbourhead was evacuated. The R.A.F. personnel and the Police wre on guard but no one in those days even considered the possibility of looting. In fact those evacuated were told to leave their doors and windows open, because it would cause less damage, if the plane exploded.

The police phoned Mr. Johnson to confirm that the plane had been identified as being from R.A.F. Marham and that there were twelve 500 lbs. bombs on board. After the ammunition had all been spent, the fire was eventually extinguished and people were allowed to return home but the road remained closed for five weeks, while a squad of twelve men from the Bomb Disposal Unit made all the bombs safe. They had to dig down twenty feet to reach some of them.

Mr. Johnson instructed the children to hand in anything they found later in the vicinity and amongst the items collected were the radio operator's manual and the identity plates of the pilot, Capt. Norman Hunt and the bomber, W.J. Hession. These were returned to R.A.F. Marham and Mr. Johnson later made contact with Capt. Hunt's parents and told them all he knew of the circumstances of their son's death.

During the war Mr. Clark, who now lives in Woad Farm Road, lived in a house near Kelsey Bridge on the Sibsey Road. He remembers a German Junkers bomber being shot down and crash-landing in a field down Pilley's Lane. The crew survived but surrendered to the farmer and members of a Home Guard patrol.

                                    13 July 1944
                                    Target, Saarbrucken

Crew Aboard.

        Pilot: N.J. Hunt
        Co-Pilot: P.R. Roetzel
        Bomb: W.J.Hession
        Eng: W.L. McKinzie
        Rad. Oper: H.C. Wilkinson
        Nose Gunn: W.E. Caurington
        Rt. Wst. Gunn: M. Osment
        Lt. Wst. Gunn: D.L. McEwan
        Tail Gunn: L.A. Jackson

Takeoff at 5.30a.m. in rain and heavy overcast.
We had icing conditions for awhile but the ice
soon left and the aircraft resumed normal flight.
A few minutes later the ice reappeared - this
time the aircraft - including the propellers was
covered with very heavy ice and the propellers
"ran away" and the aircraft was out of control.

At this time I attempted to leave through the
waist window but was caught half-in and half-out
and was semi-conscious from striking the side of
the aircraft. A few seconds later I was thrown
clear, pulled the ripcord and then lost
consciousness.

I regained consciousness on the ground. I
remember talking to two children and members of
the British Home Guard. I was placed on an
ironing board and transported to a RAF Hospital.

Report of D.L. McEwan, sole survivor of the plane that crashed at
Wrangle Bank on 13th July 1944.

ALL PRESENT, SKIP

In 1944 I joined the 5th. Boston Scout Troop and became a member of the Kingfisher Patrol, standing at the end of the line behind my brother, Jim, his friend, Ken Johnson, Pud Payton, Donkey Warren and Patrol Leader, Ray Issit. The Scout Master was Skip Lucas, who I already knew, as he lived in a small house between Lincoln Lane and Station Street, just before Parker's Yard. Parkers were then undertakers; they started boat-building a few years after the war. I often saw Skip, when I visited my grandmother in Station Street.

Over the years I moved up the line, as older boys left and I eventually became Patrol Leader. When I joined, the Troop Leader was Bill Westkin, who lived at Wyberton but he left town and Ray Issit was promoted to Troop Leader. Ray was an athletic leader and we all emulated him. The troop grew, while Ray was Skip Lucas's right-hand man and he was sorely missed, when in the fullness of time he became a paratrooper.

One Sunday each month we went on Church Parade, visiting in time every church and chapel in the area. We would assemble at our headquarters and march through the streets. At that time I could recognise the interior of any religious venue within marching distance of Boston. I could not help but notice the extremes between a small spartan chapel and an ornate high church but the reverence was just as sincere in each.

Our headquarters was an old building on the Pack House Quay in South Street. It was pulled down long ago and the site is now a car park. It came just before Lincoln's Seed Warehouse, which is now the Sam Newsom Music Centre. Our meetings were held upstairs and the wooden floors did little to hide the noise of thirty or forty pairs of feet, as we paraded in our patrols.

All the patrols were given bird's names; Curlew, Blackbird, Raven, Kiwi etc. One of the patrols consisted mainly of the Mitchell brothers: Gordon, the eldest was

67

patrol leader, then there were two sets of twins, Tony and Terry, then Jack and Gerry, who was known to everyone as Buster. Tony and Terry were identical twins but Jack had straight dark hair, while Gerry had lighter curly hair. Jack achieved local fame, as a racing cyclist but Gerry died young, as the result of an accident, while working at Wings down Woodthorpe Avenue, when he fell in a vat of boiling fat.

Boys left, as they grew older, and new recruits appeared but for various reasons the following have found a place in my memory: Peter Stevens, Tom Bridges, Malcolm Penson, Jacky Redmile, Peter Thompson, Tom Redman, Peter Blanchard, Bill Inman, who became Troop Leader, when Ray Issit left, and Robin Everett. Robin started with me in the Kingfisher Patrol but was later Patrol Leader of the Ravens. After I left the scouts, he was Troop Leader for many years.

Jacky Redmile, who went to live in Southern Rhodesia, was adept at writing parodies. Skip Lucas organised shows to raise funds and on one occasion we all persuaded our parents and friends to buy tickets for an evening of songs and sketches at the Mission To Seaman Hall at the Dock gates. Jacky wrote a parody of "There's a long, long trail a winding", which proved successful. His version went: "There's a long, long worm a crawling, Across the roof of my tent. The early caller's bawling And it's time I went. There's some cold. cold water waiting For me to take my morning dip And, when I return, I'll find that worm upon my pi-illow slip."

In the final sketch I appeared as an elderly maid with my face blackened and well padded. I had recently seen "Gone With The Wind", so I tried to sound like Hattie McDaniel and I must have done fairly well, because my mother told me later that, as they went home, my father wondered why I had not been in the show. He didn't recognise me.

Several times a year, on important occasions, there were parades through the market place to the Stump. Skip Lucas always tried to make sure that we outsmarted and outmarched the other Scout Troop, led by Skip Austin and the Sea Scouts, under their leader, Mr. Twiddy. There was a friendly rivalry between the three troups.

The parade was led by either the Army Cadets, the Air Cadets or George Wilson's Boys' Brigade, as they all had bands. The Home Guard with Jimmy Ward out in front were always in the Parade together with the various A.R.P. units and sometimes an attachment from R.A.F. Coningsby. Depending on the weather, the market place was usually crowded and the Stump was full.

The Rev. P.E. Mann, who held a post at St. Botolphs and took R.I. lessons at the Grammar School, was also a Scoutmaster and he sometimes accompanied us, when we went camping. His favourite camp-fire rendering was the "Trek-cart Song.

Scouts today travel miles, even abroad, to camps and jamborees but we had to be satisfied with somewhere within marching distance. One year we camped in a field not far from Kirton Church and for me it was jinxed.

To open the camp the flag was raised and we all stood around the flag and repeated the Scouts' pledge of honour. On the flag were the words "God save the King". When I was young, I was a little short-tongued, so, when I loudly read the words, it sounded like "God shave the King", which raised gales of laughter and earned me the sobriquet of "shaver".

Not a very good start but worse was to come. While most scouts were pitching the tents, a small working party were detailed by Skip to dig the latrenes. He chose well as far as the digging was concerned, for the hole was both wide and deep but he picked the wrong lad to find the piece of wood to support the occupier's weight, while the latrene was in use.

It must have gradually weakened everytime it was used but, of course, I was the unfortunate victim, when it decided to snap in two. I was recovering from this mishap and had reached the point, where I was allowed back in the tent, when Skip announced it was time to play rounders.

The six patrols divided into two teams and our team batted first. I waited frustratingly at the back of a line of impatient batsmen, until eventually the lad in front on me faced the bowler. I had been admiring his physique for the last half an hour and thinking it was a good job he was on our side but I was soon to change my mind.

He took an almighty swipe at the ball, missed it but continued his swing and hit me on the forehead. I must have been too close to him but not for long; I was thrown back a good five yards.

I never did have my turn at batting: in fact I never knew who won or even if the game was finished. All I remember was Skip telling someone to rub my forehead with butter and a voice saying "What will we put on the bread?" When I came round my skin felt tight and I had acquired a beautiful egg-shaped bump over my left eye.

I recall little more about that camp, except the feeling of utter relief, when I finally reached the safety of home.

One Sunday in 1945 there was a Garden Fete at Frampton Hall, which at that time was the home of Mr. Frank Dennis. A statue of his father, William Dennis, stands in front of the Town Hall in Kirton.

Frank Dennis had led an interesting life. During the First World War he had bought the Peacock & Royal Hotel in Boston Market Place, when the owners went bankrupt, and he used the hotel to provide accomodation for female landworkers.

When the Conservative Member of Parliament for the Holland Division, Arthur Wellesley Dean, died in February, 1929, Frank Dennis stood in the resulting by-election as an Independent Agriculturist, because he did not agree with the Government's agricultural policy.

Our troup was asked to help prepare the grounds at Frampton Hall for the fete and return the following day to restore the status quo. To us in 1945 Frank Dennis was just a very kind host, who appreciated our help, when help was hard to find. Both he and his son, Peter, impressed us with their unpatronising treatment of both us and their staff to such an extent that three of us went there most weekends that summer and helped the butler and gardener with their chores.

Tommy Bridges was one of my companions. He lived in Church Street and was an expert at planning adventures. One Sunday, when we were not needed at Frampton Hall, he planned that we should walk from Boston to Spilsby. It sounded a good idea at the time and I fancied the view from the top of Keal Hill.

We did not reach Spilsby; we did not reach Keal Hill; we did not even reach Sibsey. He decided to rest a while, when we reached the Pied Bull, and we ate the lunch our mothers had packed for us, waited for it to digest, then walked home again.

Looking back I can never remember consciously deciding to leave the Scouts; it may have been, when I joined the Combined Cadet Force at the Grammar School or I just missed a few meetings and gradually my landyard, kneckerchief and woggle, together with my shirt with it's short sleeves heavy with badges my mother had sewn on, were taken out of the drawer less and less. Other interests usurp your time without your being aware.

Scouts of the Kingfisher Patrol (left to right): Ken Johnson, Jim Mould.

IT MIGHT NEVER HAPPEN

Fortunately many of the preparations at the start of the war never had to be implemented in Boston but plans were made for any emergency. If there had ever been a really bad air raid with large numbers injured and others left homeless and without food, temporary shelter would have been available at the Congregational Schoolroom in Red Lion Square and the Adult School in Liquorpond Street.

The local Public Assistance Committee were required by the Ministry of Health to prepare a scheme, known as the Prevention and Relief of Distress Scheme. A Relieving Officer was appointed to make sure that both establishments had a constant supply of iron rations, consisting of biscuits, chocolate, tinned soup, tea etc. and contingency plans to procure at short notice such perishable items as bread and cheese.

Facilities had to be organised for making tea and soup and having on hand hurricane lamps for emergency lighting. Other buildings were provisionally earmarked for use, if necessary.

There was also an Emergency Hospital Scheme, which was administered jointly by the County Council's Public Health and Public Assistance Depaertments. The County Medical Officer dealt with the engagement of doctors and nurses, while the Public Assistance Officer organised the administration and obtained the equipment and supplies.

All hospitals were graded. Boston General Hospital was Grade 1A, as it could perform all classes of work but Spalding Hospital was Grade 1B, because it was not so well equipped. Smaller establishments, such as the Isolation Hospital, the Institutions and the Convalescent Homes, were either Grade 2 or Grade 3. The Ministry of Health supplied collapsible beds to br set up at any establishment, where there was insufficient accomodation at any time.

Animals were not forgotten: there was a local office of N.A.R.P.A.C. in High Street, where the Chief Organiser was

A.H. Carnegy-Capel and the Chief Veterinary Officer was A. Anderson Walker. The secretary was Miss Doris Kirk, who, after the war, was the local secretary of the R.A.F. Association.

The same ten areas that applied to air raid wardens each had a Chief Animal Guard and there were five first aid posts for animals.

They say "Don't worry, it might never happen." and luckily in Boston it didn't but it did in many towns and, if it had here, Boston was well prepared.

LET'S PLAY "MURDER"

Apart from Bedford's Mill there was another fire during the war, that had no connection with bombs. This time there was no audience, as it happened in the middle of the night. The St. Botolph's Youth Fellowship had a clubroom on the Doughty Quay, next door to William's newspaper shop, which had a full-sized Billiards table in one of the ground floor rooms.

Another room was used for games and on the night of the fire a group of lads, including George Bell and Jack "Donkey" Bray had been playing cards. Everything was in order, when they locked up and went home but in the early hours fire broke out and the whole building was destroyed. The cause of the fire was never established.

It left the Youth Fellowship without a clubroom but one was found much nearer to the Church. The property at the corner of Wormgate and Fountain Lane, which is now Staniland's wallpaper shop, was vacant and it became their new clubroom.

A Billiards table was installed in the long room downstairs and there were two table tennis tables upstairs. In addition to club nights during the school holidays, a crowd of boys and girls spent hours there during the daytime. Rev. David Cartwright was in charge but, of course, he could not be there all the time.

My sister, Audrey and her lifelong friend, Doreen Bycroft, were members and I remember several of those, she came home and told us about: Lavinia Whalley, Rosemary Brown, Madge Smith, Valerie Kinsey, Carol Chesman, Winsome Smith and Margaret Loveley. She also entertained us with tales about the following boys: Maurice Dawson, Gordon Tait, Derek Holdsworth, George and Peter Bell, Robin Midgeley and Johnny Britton, who later went to London and appeared in several West End plays and had a small part in the film "The Battle of the River Plate".

Audrey and Doreen both met their future husbands there;

Johnny Colam and Dick Ryan.

One of the favourite games they played, when enough people were there, was "murder". They all drew a card out of a hat and one person was the murderer and one was the victim. The victim had to chose the place, where his or her body was to be found and, after they had found the body, the murderer had to be discovered.

The building was ideal for this purpose, as there were numerous rooms, including some attics. One day they had just started a game and Doreen Bycroft was the victim; she went into an attic to hide but it did not take long for the others to find "the body", for she had fallen through the ceiling and at least half the body was exposed immediately.

Lifelong Friends: (left to right): Audrey Colam (Mould), Doreen Ryan (Bycroft)

IN THE SPRING THE SAP RISES

Many of the younger masters at the Grammar School were in the forces, so, when I became a pupil there in 1944, several lady teachers were deputising. Mrs. Brough, who introduced me to French, had a distinctive walk: she bounced down the corridors, almost as if she were on the Cake Walk. She was a very good teacher and made French grammar easy to understand. It was only after I left school, that I realised she was a celebrated local artist and exhibitions of her paintings were often arranged.

My first English teacher was also a lady. Mrs. Jakes was efficient and she was the first in a line of teachers, who encouraged and nurtured my interest in the written word. Mrs. Wilkinson had literally replaced her husband and she was our Geography teacher. She was very tall and had no difficulty observing those at the back of the class.

I had no first-hand experience of the other two lady teachers. Mrs. Morris, the Headmaster's wife, taught Science and I am not sure of Mrs. Collins's subject. She was the youngest and most glamorous of the ladies and I understand the boys in the front desk made a habit of dropping their pencils.

Doc Morris, the Headmaster, taught Religious Instruction and he was liked and revered by all the boys. Unfortunately he left in 1945 and I did not have time to appreciate his sterling qualities. My brother had started the Grammar School in 1942 and he often regaled in telling me how Doc Morris at morning assembly infused his pupils with this statement: "The war is not yet over; we must put every ounze of strength into our efforts." He emphasised the word ounze by punching forward at an invisible enemy and often lost his balance.

Captain Morris had an artificial leg, a legacy of his war service. He came to the Grammar School directly from the First World War and brought with him his batman, Sam Wray, who became the caretaker, and a sergeant, who had served under him, Mr. Burton. The sports field down

Church Road was the domain of Mr. Burton. He always wore black gaiters and must have been the smartest groundsman in the county.

Dick Parkinson, who later was to distinguish himself in both the school cricket and football teams, lived in Church Road, when the war started, and with other boys he followed Mr. Burton during the football season, as he marked all the pitches immaculately with bold white lines.

During his lunch break, which he spent in a corrugated shed in the far right-hand corner of the field, he plied the boys with Fox's Glazier Mints, of which he always seemed to have a supply.

The pavillion was always kept neat and tidy and the paling fence enclosing it always appeared freshly painted. Summer was Mr. Burton's favourite season, for then he was in his element preparing the Square, hallowed ground which he would mow meticulously for the Saturday match. There would sometimes be a special match in mid-week and, if it were thought the pavillion would not hold all the visitors, Mr. Burton would supervise the erection of a marquee for refreshments.

Joe Gledhill, the Latin master, lived in Church Road and he organised nets and fielding practise every Thursday evening during the cricket season. Before the lads hurried away to tackle their home-work, a horse-drawn roller was used on the pitch and they replaced the horses.

I did not take Latin, so I never came in direct contact with Mr. Gledhill but I often heard other boys tell of his particular method of punishment, the dreaded "little benjamin", which I understand was a special ruler he used to rap boys over the knuckles.

I did experience "Tilly" Turpin's speciality. He used an elastic band: he would walk round the class, while we were writing in our exercise books, then suddenly he would flick someone behind the ear. It was not too painful but the uncertainty of just when and where he would strike, affected some boy's nerves. In fact Michael Priestley often broke into tears, as soon as he entered the room and, like a boxer playing on a weakness, "Tilly" picked on him unmercifully. It was not wise to watch too closely, if you could see him taking aim at a certain innocent ear, for occasionally he would let the other end of the band go and threaten the eye of anyone behind. Mr. Turpin was a very keen painter and his artistic flair expressed itself in other ways. One year he was our form master and on the first day of term he stood on his desk and moved us around the classroom according to the colour of our hair to form a pattern that pleased his artist's eye.

"Binky" Border, the senior Maths teacher, was also Deputy Headmaster. He had been a Major in the First World War and was extremely frustrated, when he was told he was too old to take part in 1939. I admired him greatly, for he was able to control a class without using any force and never resorted to sarcasm. I once witnessed his method of putting a point across with the upmost effect but with the least fuss.

"Froggy" Howes, the veteran French teacher was walking laboriously along the corridor, for he had trouble with his legs and could not hurry. Some first-formers were walking behind and mocking him. "Binky" came up quietly behind them and made them look even smaller than they were. He told them that the man they chose to ridicule was an Amateur International and in his younger days had played centre forward for England.

Like Mr. Chips, "Froggy" Howes had been ready to retire, when the war started but he was persuaded to stay on as the senior French teacher. His nasal tone was perfect for sounding the different French accents and he brought his own style of comic relief to the classroom. He could always see the funny side of anything. For example one day my brother's class were translating a passage from a French book into English. It was something to do with the seasons and their effect on trees. Each boy in turn translated a few lines and just as "Tubby" Ellis stood up to ask to leave the room, the boy translating said "In the spring the sap rises." Froggy laughed to himself and commented: "Yes indeed, the sap rises."

On another occasion "Froggy" asked Peter Howes in my class, if he liked lemonade. He appreciated the joke, when Peter answered ungrammatically "Non, non mon belle ami." (At the time Bellamy's pop was one of the most popular brands.)

"Snoddy" Deighton was the German teacher: his gown was always in shreds and he spent half of each period staring out of the window or into space; it was hard to tell where his thoughts were centred. The other half of the lesson must have been put to good use, for I gained a distinction in German in my School Certificate and I can still recite Die Lorelei from start to finish.

"Titch" Collins also taught German but he only ever took our form for Religious Instruction. His lessons were always interesting, because he called on his experiences as a missionary in Africa to illustrate religious points.

From his nickname you would have expected "Fritz" Wheeler to have taught German but his subject was actually mathematics. He had two fingers missing and he used to prod his victim with the stump, shouting "Yew Boy, Yew Boy." His voice was reminiscent of a Gestapo officer. We all had difficulty understanding him and our maths suffered accordingly.

When he left, the position became even worse, for he was replaced by Mr. McNeil, who was possibly a good teacher but we were never able to find out, because his broad Scottish accent was wasted on our sassanach ears. He was soon known throughout the school as "McNab" and became one of the few teachers, who experienced trouble controlling his class.

There is little wonder that Maths was my worse subject and, those in our year, who did well in their school certificate, could only have had "Tusker" Tonks to thank. He only took us for one year but all we knew we learned in that year. He was the strictest teacher in the school and no one talked or wasted time during his period. His appearance made small boys tremble: he was the heaviest teacher by far and his face and neck became red, when his temper was roused.

Victor Emery and myself had reason to verify this one afternoon, when we returned from lunchtime and found our entrance into the classroom barred by other boys holding the door. We were both well-built and soon forced our way in then we made the fateful decision to hold the door fast against the next boy. The rest of the class shared our amusement, when he could not enter the room but we realised they were laughing at us not with us, when it dawned on us that all the desks were full and we were blocking Mr. Tonks's path. He was not called "Tusker" for nothing, for, as we made an impossible attempt to reach our desks, he charged in like a bull elephant and the veins on his forehead and in his neck stood out, like a fireman's hose throbbing into action. I tasted fear that afternoon and the memory will never fade but I will always regard him with respect and admiration.

Ironically it was mathematics that indirectly caused his downfall. He was appointed treasurer of the local British Legion and found guilty of embezzling the funds. Ernie Ancliff, who was in my brother's form, joined the prison service and on his first day at Wakefield prison he walked into a cell and there was "Tusker" Tonks. How are the mighty fallen?

Another teacher fell foul of the law: Bill Bastick was the senior English master and once again he would not tolerate bad behaviour. I understand he was a good teacher and his pupils were encouraged to appreciate Shakespeare but he never taught me, so my memories of him are restricted to seeing him walking down the corridors with his hand holding his gown across the chest.   His face also had a healthy glow but in his case it illustrated his appreciation of liquid refreshment.   Strange that the two sternest disciplinarians were the same two, who went astray.

Gaffer Dickson was in charge of the Science block but again I have no personal memories of him, as he was never faced with the problem of stirring my interest in either Physics or Chemistry.   As soon as it were possible I dropped a science subject and in the Cambridge, when I was fifteen, I just took Physics with Chemistry as one exam. Mr. Dickson became deputy headmaster, when "Binky" Border retired.

"Laddy" Lockwood was my science teacher for two years, until Ben Warman came out of the forces.   "Laddy", so called because of his favourite exclamation: "Oh Lad", was in charge of the School Orchestra and was a virtuoso on the violin.   My overriding memory of being in his class concerns the last day of term, before breaking up for the Christmas holidays.   I believe he used the same routine with every class but, at least, it was more entertaining that most teacher's efforts to ease into the festive spirit.

He drew pictures on the blackboard and we had to guess which proverb they represented.   The one that most boys remember, when I broach the subject, was where he drew three perches and marked them G-H, M-N and S-T, then he drew a parrot on each of them but the parrot on G-H was just a rough outline, on M-N it was in more detail but the parrot on S-T was a work of art, taking him much longer to finish.   He was very happy, if no one could decipher the proverb, and took real pleasure in explainig that: "On S-T is the best Pol I see".

The teacher, who experienced the most difficulty in controlling his class was Mr. Ferguson, the Art master.   He was not cut out to force thirty-five lively lads, the majority of whom had no great pretensions of becoming either a Turner or a Picasso, to concentrate on art throughout his period. His dilemma reached a climax one day, when one of the more unruly pupils threatened him with a knife (Yes, such things happened occasionally even in those days) and, although the culprit was expelled, he did not feel he could face the torment any longer. His successor, Mr. Grimmond, was a much more challenging proposition to the trouble-makers and those looking for a relief of tension from more important subjects were left with one channel only.

Dr.Bernard Jackson was for many years organist at St. Botolph's Church and, unfortunately for him, he was also our Music teacher. The music classroom was situated above the Masters' Commonroom, as far away as possible from the rest of the school, so the unmelodious wailing caused minimum nuisance.

In keeping control "Jacko" had the added handicap of playing the piano with his back to the class. His most amusing and magnetic feature was the tufts of hair growing horizontally out of both ears. One day, while we were rendering "Nymphs and Shepherds Come Away" and he was lost in the music, one daring lad could resist the challenge no longer. He crept behind Dr. Jackson and set fire to the hairs protruding from his left ear with a lighter and managed to regain his seat and adopt an innocent expression, before the alarmed "Jacko" turned round.

The consequences of the miscreant's derring-do were that Dr. Jackson had to visit the barber in haste to restore equilibrium by having the still rampant hairs removed from his right ear and also that the piano, rather belatedly, was moved to prevent anyone ever again approaching unnoticed.

The master I knew best was Mr. Cox, the senior Geography teacher. He lived with his charming wife in a bungalow near the top of Tytton Lane East and they were customers on my father's bread round. On Saturdays and during the school holidays I delivered their bread, while my father went to a house opposite. I still remember their regular order: a small white and a hovis. All through he war he cherished and maintained his immaculate car and ran it for many years, after the war.

They were the kindest and most considerate couple you could wish to meet and I never liked to see boys mock him or play games on him but I needed have worried, for he was more than capable of looking after himself. The boys always referred to him as "Curious" Mr. Cox, because he was apt to exclaim, when presented with a wrong answer: "Curious, curious, I wouldn't have known!"

Although elderly, he was very fit and usually wore plimsoles and was one of the most active teachers on Sport's Day. He was also in charge of the Grammar School's meteorological department and took readings each day from the weather hut in the middle of the quadrangle, where the four paths met. One morning, after a night of steady rain, some boys decided to try and fool him. They filled the rain container to the brim but not with water.

When Mr. Cox appeared to take his readings, he noticed more boys than usual observing his routine, some with smirks on their faces, so, without giving them the pleasure of hearing him utter even one "curious", he called one boy across, whom he correctly assessed to be the ringleader, and told him to take the container to the toilets, where it belonged, and wash it out thoroughly. After that episode the weather hut was always secured with a lock.

Mr. Dowson was the new French teacher, when "Froggy" Howes retired and he safely manoeuvred us through our oral and written exams. He seems to be almost the only teacher I can remember, who was not blessed with a sobriquet and I can recall no anecdote concerning him but maybe others will.

In 1945, when "Doc" Morris retired, "Snag" Waddams became the Headmaster. The contrast could not have been more marked: the one respected by all and remembered with affection; the other creeping round the corridors reminiscent of Caesar's remark: "Yon Cassius has a lean and hungry look." Throughout my schooling all the teachers I encountered earned my respect: they had varying degrees of success in shaping my future or improving my intellect but they all made a honest and fair attempt. The exception was Mr. Waddams; his main concern was to try to cast doubt on every boys endeavours, instead of encouraging them to strive for greater achievements.

CLASS OF '44

Six girls and six boys moved on from Staniland School to the High School and Grammar School in 1944.

The girls were: Barbara Blackwell, Pamela Kinsey, Margaret Lacey, Pat ladds, Janet Midgelow and Janet Troops and the boys were: Gordon Butcher, Peter Day, Victor Emery, Noel Holgate, Peter Luff and myself.

Only one school had a better pass rate: Park Board had nine girls and an astonishing seventeen boys. The boys were: Gordon Barker, John Cammack, Geoff Cross, Robin Everett, Gary Gerson, Peter Howes, Norman Kinsey, Joe Lovelace, Ralph Mashford, Dick Parker, Malcolm Penson, Ron Ruskin, Derek Simmonds, Jack Sleight, Barry Smith, Derek Whelbourn and Jim Wightman.

Butterwick was the next most successful school that year, although no girls qualified, they had six boys: Sid Bushby, Alan Curtis, Derek Fox, John Gosling, Stan Graves and Richard Taylor. The others came from: St. Thomas's; Tony Brown, Bryn Johnson, St. Botolph's; Jim Ransom, Brian Redman, Fishtoft; Tony Harrison, John Harrison, Tower Road; Geoff Thorlby, Old Leake; Aubrey West, Charles Wright, Kirton Holme; Mick Barnfield, Geoff Dunham and Kirton; Arnold Cooper, John Faulkner.

The following boys had been paid for and had already been at the Grammar School for two years: Philip Cooper, Tony Jakes, Derek Marshall, Rodney Newell, Michael Priestley, Jim Sargent and Brian Wrigley.

I have a list of all the children, who won scholarships or "special places" in 1944, issued by the Education Committee of the Holland County Council. There were 399 candidates, 222 girls and 177 boys. Of these 81 girls passed and 92 boys. Many of these went to Spalding Grammar and High Schools.

For some reason a few of my classmates are not included, so I can not be sure, which elementary school they attended. They are Ken Cross, Maurice Choat, Eric Slinger and Don Smith.

There were two late arrivals: Robin Frost joined us, when his father came to Boston as the Chief of Police and Mick Andrews missed the first term or two.

As I write, I know seven of the class have died and the whereabouts of several others are unknown. Mick Barnfield emigrated to Australia with his family, while we were still at school. His father was the Headmaster at Kirton Holme school and Commandant of a local unit of Army Cadets. Gary Gershon, a dentist's son moved to London, after two years and Robin Frost left Boston, when his father moved on but he was replaced by Geoff Hasted, the son of the Chief Fire Officer. Jim Wightman moved to Spalding shortly before we took the School Certificate examinations.

Gordon Butcher, who had been with me at Staniland, was killed during our first year. He was a cheerful, friendly boy with bright red hair and he was cycling home from school one afternoon, when he was knocked off his bicycle and fell under the back wheels of a coal-lorry at the top of Frampton Place.

The bad news spread quickly but it was not until the Headmaster announced his death at assembly the next morning that I could actually believe it and his empty desk that day was a poignant proof for us all.

Joe Lovelace was the tallest boy in the class in 1944, wearing "long-uns", while most of us still had short trousers, but by 1949 he was one of the smallest. He played centre forward that first year, as he had this height advantage and he headed all his goals but, as others grew level with him and passed him, he still kept his position but adapted himself, so that he now scored by dribbling through the opposing defense. He died soon after leaving school.

Peter Howes became one of my best friends at school. His parents had the vegetable stall in the market near Fosters; his brother Dick carried it on, when they died. Peter was a jazz fanatic and developed his love of traditional jazz, when Freddy Randall and Mick Mulligan with George Melly were regular visitors to the Gliderdrome. We spent a week together in London to celebrate our success in the School Certificate and every night we attended a different jazz club. Peter knew them all: Ronnie Scott's was a new venue then but it is still going strong. Even on the Sunday night we went out of town to the Crooks Ferry Inn.

Peter's other love was cards: we were both members of a Brag school, that held regular meetings in the loft above my father's garage. If it were the weekend or school holidays and we could settle down to a long session, we started with nine card brag and all three hands had to be won but we always switched to three card brag for the last two hours and the Cincinnati Kid was nowhere in it.

The other members of the brag school were Curly Sharp, Beatty Smith, Mick Clayton and John Clark. The five of us played so often that we knew each other's bluff and double bluff methods intimately. It was almost impossible to prevent the others knowing, when you had a prisle of threes; you had to hope someone else had a prisle of aces.

I lost touch with Peter, when he went to the University of California and I had a terrible shock, when I noticed a brief announcement in the Lincolnshire Standard that he had died.

Mick Clayton also died, even younger; he suffered from ashma all his life and often had to use an inhaler. His mother had a sweet shop in High Street, next door to Creasey's butchers shop and, after he left the Grammar School, Mick worked at Parson' Coal Yard near the station, then later at Johnson's Seeds in the office. He was a little younger than me but we became close friends and soon after I married I was pleased to hear he was engaged but he had a chronic attack one Saturday morning and died, before he actually married.

Bryan "Curly" Sharp was a year behind me at the Grammar School, in the same class as Lou Brooks, Maurice Judge, Peter Jordan, Gordon Upsall, Pete Lovley, Alan Williams and George Wheatman. He joined Hardy & Collins, when he left school and has recently retired, after being a sales associate for many years with Allied Dunbar.

John Clark achieved local fame, as Captain of Boston Cricket Club and played for Lincolnshire. His reputation as a slow, left-arm bowler reaches much further and he still turns out regularly. He also shares the distinction with Hugh Pinner of being the only two players to have been both Town Snooker and Town Billiards Champions.

Barry Trevor "Beatty" Smith completed the card school; like Peter Howes he was in my class at the Grammar School but he did not travel as far from Boston. The last I heard he was teaching at a private school in North Lincolnshire, after gaining his degree at Durham University. We were walking home one night, after a strenuous evening of table tennis and Beatty complained of terrible stomach pains. He was rushed to hospital and they operated immediately. His appendix had burst and he had peritonitus.

When Derek "Mort"Marshall left school, he trained as a projectionist at the Odeon and I heard nothing more of him, until I again read in the Lincolnshire Standard that he had died. Jim Sargent's death was on the front page, for he was killed in a road accident, as he was driving into Boston from his business at Frithville.

I saw Ralph "Tashy" Mashford at least twice a year, when our Billiards teams played each other. He was in charge of maintenance at the Pilgrim Hospital. His elder brother, John, played in the same Billiards team, first at St. James's Club, then at the Conservative Club. They were both very popular and the League was saddened, when John died, then a few years later Ralph died as well. Our deep feelings of loss must have been dwarfed by his mother's grief. Mrs. Mashford was a kind, cheerful lady, who for many years ran the New Way Library, which used to occupy one of the front rooms of the White Hart, next to the river. Her eldest son, Tom, never played Billiards but he was well known locally, as a drummer in the dance bands.

I only heard recently that a seventh member of our class had died. John Faulkner from Kirton, who spent most of his life in the Royal Navy died at his home in Hampshire a few months ago. At school he was one of the most self-confident boys; "Tilly" Turpin never picked on John, when he was choosing a victim.

Most boys had nick-names: for obvious reasons John was known as "Forky" and I was "Mouldy", then some derived from initials, such as "Katie" Cross and "Beatty" Smith and "Ham" Priestley from his second christian name, Ambrose. Bryn "Cow" Johnson earned his from his incessant use of his favourite expression: "Oh you cow". Of some, however, I never did discover the origin. Why Derek Fox was called "Milky", why John Cammack was always "Bunty", where did Rodney Newell pick up his sobriquet "Croaker" or why Richard Taylor was known by everyone as "Quack". In fact, until I received the list of successful 1944 candidates, I did not realise his proper name was Richard.

A few of the class left Great Britain: apart from Mick Barnfield emigrating to Australia, Jim Ransom went to Southern Rhodesia and is now settled in South Africa and Peter Howes and Victor Emery both went to the University of California. More about Vic later.

At least two joined the Church. Geoff Cross became a Methodist minister and settled in South-West England, after leaving the active ministry. Geoff, like "Beatty" Smith went to Durham University, as did Robin Everett, who was ordained in Leicester in 1959, after completing his National

Service and returning to Durham to receive his B.A. degree. The Rev. Robin N. Everett is now the Rector of Ibstock and Heather: he has remained in the Leicester diocese for 36 years and retires in 1998.

He married Ruth Dann at the Stump in 1960 and they have a son in Nottingham and a daughter, who lives in Derby, so they have no plans to return to Boston. As I have mentioned previously Robin was also in the scouts with me and his sister, Mavis, was a Girls Guide leader most of her life but, unfortunately, she died a few years ago.

During 1986-87 Robin spent twelve months in Montserrat, near Antigua in the West Indies and returned in 1991 to help the islanders clear up after Hurricane Hugo. They are still in his thoughts and prayers, as they are now threatened by a possible eruption of a volcano, that has been dormant for two hundred years.

While Robin was Vicar of Castle Donington in the 1970s, he met Brian Wrigley, who had been working for Rolls-Royce in Derby but was about to move on. Robin reminded me that Brian was John Cammack's cousin.

Jim Wightman, who moved to Spalding Grammar School prior to taking the School Certificate exams, became a medical practitioner and eventually ran a surgery at Ancaster. He retired in 1995 and now lives at The Old Rectory, Welby, near Grantham.

Tony Jakes became an Airline Pilot, flying jet planes over the Atlantic, then for years Channel-hopping for a holiday and freight company. He now lives in Farnham and I spoke with him in 1995, when he returned to Boston for a few weeks, while his mother was ill in the Pilgrim Hospital, His mother was George Brocklesby's sister and was a director of Brocklesby's Mineral Waters, who traded for many years near the top of Rosegarth Street. When I visited Tony, while we were at school, I admired his mother's fine house at the top of Irby Street and in 1995 she was again living in a beautiful home; one of the flats that Adrian Isaac has built near his moated house behind Spilsby Road.

Tony's father was a sergeant in the Police Force before the war but was killed, while on traffic duty in 1935. Bertram Mills's circus came to Boston and their Big Top was raised in Mountain's field down Sleaford Road. Sergeant Jakes was controlling the traffic at the end of their performance and a vehicle caught him and dragged him along the road.

Derrick Simmon's father, George, played for Boston United, when the Midland League was re-formed after the war. Derrick was an enthusiastic footballer but his brother, Colin, was the more gifted player and ran on to many of the balls I booted upfield, when I played left back for the Old Boys and he played inside right. I recently received a letter from John Crabb, thanking me for stirring old memories in my column, and he told me that Derrick is fit and well and living not far from John's home in Beverley.

I have crossed paths with many of the class in the forty-five years, since we left school that summer and threw our caps in the air (I had to retrieve mine, as I was returning to the sixth form.) but I have neither seen nor heard any news of the following: Gordon Barker, Arnold Cooper, Ken Cross, Maurice Choat, Derek Fox, John Gosling, Tony Harrison, Bryn Johnson, Malcolm Penson and Richard Taylor. If any of you read this or if anyone has news of any of them, please let me know and I shall be very grateful.

I do not know the present whereabouts of Brian Rodney "Croaker" Newell but for a while he featured on the pages of the Lincolnshire Standard, when he was trying to make contact with his estranged wife in order to see his children. Even at school Rodney, as I always called him, was more mature than most of the class. In fact I believe he became engaged to Enid Newton, while in the fifth form.

He was a cross between Errol Flynn and David Niven, an

expert at both action and conversation. His blonde, curly hair was irresistible to the fair sex and the boys crowded round him every morning to hear tales of his conquests from the previous night and sometimes to see proof, for he was also an advanced photographer and could set up a camera at remarkable angles, so he featured in the photographs himself.

When he married Lindis Perkins, whose father had a garage at the bottom of Argyle Street, he settled down and was running the Post Office at the corner of Willoughby Road and Hospital Lane, when Lindis took the children to Australia. I never heard if he ever found them.

Although I lost track of Tony Harrison, I had news of his brother (or were they cousins), John. My sister used to speak of him, when he helped her husband, Johnny Colam, with his accounts, while he was building in Boston, before he joined the Prison Service. Audrey was always grateful to John Harrison and, coincidentally, his sister used to work in the Willoughby Road Post Office, when it belonged to Mr. and Mrs. Richmond.

Ken Cross's parents lived next door to my sister in Eastwood Road, opposite Teddy West's fish and chip shop but I never knew, if Ken stayed in Boston or not.

Of those who did stay faithful to Boston I see some regularly and others only occasionally. Philip Cooper, for example, I did encounter, when I played table tennis many years ago but the last time I saw him he was talking to one of his employees, Brian Martin, at Wrangle.

Another classmate concerned with produce, Michael Priestley, I saw last at the funeral of a great-aunt he shared with my wife. It transpired that Michael's mother and June's mother were cousins. I recently had an interesting conversation with him and it appears we both have a copy of the same family photograph, taken at the turn of the century. One thing Michael did not tell me was that he was one of the few National Servicemen in the R.A.F., who qualified to fly jet planes. So he has something in common with Tony Jakes. The lad, who was terrified by "Tilly" Turpin, had the last laugh.

It was Charles "Chuck" Wright, who told me about Michael's R.A.F. accomplishments and it was Charles, who entered the R.A.F. the same day as I. His father picked me up outside our shop and took us both to Spalding station, where we caught the Manchester train and made our way to Padgate. We were soon separated, because I had been in the Combined Cadet Force and was upflighted, so I missed three week's square-bashing.

We met again several years later, because June and Mary, Charles's wife, both went to Pauline's Hairdressing Salon at Wrangle and, together with June's parents, we all went to Elsam's restaurant at Horncastle and finished with a coffee at Mary's house at old Leake.

My father and "Chuck"'s father, also Charles, had worked closely together during the war, when dad was secretary and Mr. Wright was on the committee and President for one year of the Boston and District Bakers and Millers Association.

Alan Curtis worked for C.S. Johnson's, the wholesale drapers in Pump Square and, when the property was sold to Jim O'Hara and became the Snax Club, he set up his own company and continued to sell drapery, together with mens' and ladies' clothes to outlets over a wide area. He lived in a modern bungalow at Thornton-le-Fen, when last we met. His elder brother, Noel, kept the Post Office at Butterwick for many years. Alan was also a popular singer at various venues, before Karaoke was thought about.

Eric "Slosh" Slinger was another vocalist, singing with the Embassy Band. He worked with Jasper Sharp in the daytime too, repairing false teeth.

105

Geoff Dunham was a fixture in the pharmacy at Boots for many years but has recently retired. Tony Brown lived in Fydell Crescent and I was sad to see in the Lincolnshire Standard that he lost his wife at an early age. Later he became a magistrate but, although I see him quite often, we have never had the chance to converse.

Dick Parker was fearless at school, both in the classroom and on the football field. I never saw him wear shin-guards; he always played with his socks rolled down but never shirked a tackle and I can not remember him ever being hurt. His father was an undertaker down Station Street and he came to us, when my grandparents died but, when my mother died in 1969, it was Dick's wife, Joan, who came.

Dick and his brother, Bill, are now the internationally-known Parkers, the Boat Builders with premises in Horseshoe Lane, Kirton.

Brian Redman has stayed in Boston and worked most of his life at Rice, Waite & Marris, the solicitors in Main Ridge. The name of the firm is different now but Brian was still there in August, 1995, according to John Crabb. Jack Sleight was the quietest boy in the class and very rarely attracted trouble either from classmates or teachers. I would not have known he was still in Boston but for seeing photographs of the Stump choir and recognising him.

If Jack was the most introvert of our class, Don Smith was the most extravert. Most action centred around Don and many looked to him for leadership. He was well liked by all the boys and treated warily by all the teachers. On the football field he was the player, who received the most passes, as if he were carrying a magnet. He was a useful player and I was not surprised, when he had a run for Boston United on the left wing. The last time I saw him he was managing the Skegness garage for Peter Taylor but I understand he now manages the Boston Golf Club.

Aubrey West was the exact opposite of Joe Lovelace.

Whereas Joe was the tallest boy, when we started, Aubrey was the smallest but, after we left school, he shot up and finished well over six feet tall. He worked for Austin Monks, who was a famous motor cycle racer between the wars and, when he died, he left his business to his workers.

I saw Mick Andrews regularly, until he and his wife, Marjorie, sold their shop in Brothertoft Road. Marjorie ran the shop, while Mick was a television engineer. They moved to Kirton and the last time we met they were living in a caravan, while the house was being renovated. I heard recently that Mick has been forced to retire, due to his health and I am sure all his old classmates wish him well.

John Cammack has had a busy year as the Mayor's Consort and has accompanied the Mayor, his wife Judy, to numerous functions. I know he will have acquitted himself well and thoroughly enjoyed every minute, for whatever he tackled at school, and after, he always put everything into it. He is an accomplished artist: I was once admiring a painting, when we were visiting my wife's cousin and, when I looked in the corner for the artist's signature, it was signed, John Cammack.

He emulated his mother as a leading member of Boston Tennis Club and still plays table tennis. In fact he was playing at Graves Park the last time we met. I have never seen him without a smile on his face and I know I will receive a cheerful greeting whenever I notice his distinctive walk, signalling his approach.

Derek Whelbourn joined Johnson's Seeds soon after leaving school and was instrumental in their gaining the contract to provide the seed for Wembley Stadium. Alan Woodthorpe, Derek and myself ran the Old Boys' Youth team together, when we played on a pitch down the bankside at the bottom of Langrick Road. We had to be early for every match, because we had to erect the goalposts and mark the pitch, before the game could start.

Alan Woodthorpe, who worked at Fogartys but, unfortunately, died a few years ago, was one of the fastest wingers I ever saw and Derek was a skillful dribbler at inside forward, while even then my weight and build dictated that I should be a full-back.

After not seeing him for many years, I was pleased when Derek started playing snooker and turned up with Alan Ashberry for regular games at the Boston Snooker Centre. We now have the opportunity to recall those times.

I see Ron Ruskin at least twice a year, as he prints the handbook and score sheets for the local Billiards and Snooker League and I, as secretary furnish him with the fixture list and other details, then a little later I return to collect the books.

When the Midland League re-started in 1945, Ron often came home with me after Boston United's match. By then we lived at 65, High Street and we had a small snooker table in a back room on the top storey.

Ron joined his father, Len, in their printing business, when he left the Grammar School and about the same time "Chuck" Elsam started working there and they learned the trade together and became friends. Years later "Chuck" set up in business in Spalding with another lad as Cross & Elsam. They specialised in posters, printed on Heidelberg platens, replicas of those he had used at Ruskins.

Like the youths of today, we often gathered in groups and one evening about eight of us went to the Odeon to see John Wayne in "The Fighting Kentuckian". It would have been about 1950, so we were all around sixteen, going on seventeen. Chuck had a real hearty laugh and that was nearly the cause of an early exit for all of us.

The supporting film was "The Jones Family Down On The Farm" and everytime Spring Byington (Mrs. Jones) wanted Jed Prouty (Mr. Jones) she opened the farm door and shouted "Cy" at the top of her voice. The horses and cows stampeded, the pigs disappeared into their stys, the chickens ran round in circles and the family dog dived under the house. This sequence of panic tickled Chuck and it must have been repeated eight times during the film and each time his guffaws grew louder. His laughter was infectious and all eight of us were convulsed with uncontrollable merriment.

The usherette asked us to be quiet but she may as well have asked a skylark to stop singing and it was only when Mr. Pearce, the manager, threatened us with expulsion, that our laughter gradually subsided. When the main film started, I was frightened that the cacophany would re-erupt, because the man fighting at the side of John Wayne was none other than Oliver Hardy (one of only two appearances he made without Stan Laurel) but Ron sat on one side and Peter Day on the other and betwen them they kept Chuck under control.

Peter Luff had a special nick-name for me and I for him. Both our parents had the News Chronicle delivered every day and it featured a cartoon about a politician called Sir Zilliboy Shinbag. So I always called him Luffbag and he called me Mouldbag. When we were in the fifth form, we both fully intended to pursue a career in politics and enter the House of Commons. I thought Peter had actually achieved his aim, when a few years ago a Conservative M.P. called Peter Luff started to be mentioned regularly in the press. I knew Peter had entered the Foreign Office, after university, so it seemed feasible. I was really disappointed, when I saw him on television and found him to be too young for Luffbag.

At school we shared a love of organising the other boys. While I kept check of the scores and the league table for the shove-halfpenny games played every lunch-time on the master's table, Peter was busy recruiting members for his Meccano Club, which met at his house two evenings a week. Peter's father was an engine driver on the LNER and a kinder man could never be found. Mrs. Luff was very proud of Peter and sometimes embarrassed him, as she was prone to eulogize about him to all and sundry.

They both encouraged him with his Meccano Club and helped him to set-up various games in each room of their house. His club attracted many members and was a great success but he lived down Woodville Road and it was a long way from High Street, especially if, like me, you hadn't a bicycle.

Four of us faced the same problem, so one momentous day we decided to form our own club. The other three were Peter Day, Noel Holgate and Victor Emery. The loft over my father's garage was sequestrated (the same venue that later staged the brag sessions); my father's friend, Fred Parker, who worked at Edward White's Vauxhall Garage in Bargate, fixed up an electric light for us; Noel's father, Cliff Holgate, helped us whitewash the walls and make it suitable to house a table tennis table, our small snooker table and various improvised tables and chairs for monopoly, draughts etc. We were then ready for business and we soon had thirty or forty members; the fees collected went towards a royal blue football strip for our team. The shirts were plain with white collars and looked much smarter than the multi-coloured designer rubbish prevalent today. A goalkeeper almost always wore green.

The only entrance to our clubroom was up a steep ladder in the corner of dad's garage. Before he switched to Singer vans, Dad had stabled his horses in the building and their feed had been thrown down to them from the loft. There was a trap-door cover to pull across but, when lads were arriving and departing every five minutes, it was a bind to replace it each time, so it was often left open. The room was often overcrowded and we placed the various tables away from the trap-door but on two or three occasions in the heat of the moment someone either stepped back too far, while defending a table-tennis smash or just turned round while busy in conversation and disappeared down the hole.

Even today, if I talk to someone about the old clubroom, they say "Can you remember, when Tot Carter fell down the steps" or "Do you remember the night Ivor Holgate vanished through the trapdoor". Luckily, although they suffered from temporary shock, no bones were ever broken and, as far as I know, there were no repercussions in later life.

Ivor was Noel Holgate's younger brother and he was accident-prone but Tot Carter, whose father had a taxi service just over the Sleaford Road level crossing, was a small cheerful boy, who bounced back up the ladder, before anyone could go down to help him, and he was still smiling, when he rejoined us. Noel learned to pander to Ivor's every whim, because at that early age he took offence if anyone tangled with him and threw the first thing he could find and he had an unerring aim. Later Ivor experienced a conversion and became the most placid friendly person you could imagine and worked as a plumber for the corporation for years.

I have saved my three special friends and collaborators from the class of '44 till last. We all had our special talents. Noel was the musician: he played the violin and his lessons with "Laddy" Lockwood were so successful that he became first violin, therefore leader, of the School Orchestra. Every boy knew when there was to be an orchestra practise, because Fred "Schubert" Whelbourn would cycle to school with his cello strapped to his back.

Noel maintained his interest in music, after he left school, but transferred his allegiance to the double base and played with one of the local bands. For the more romantic numbers he put aside his instrument and serenaded the dancers from the front of the ensemble. The third member of the class with vocal talent.

On leaving school Noel joined Hardy & Collins as a junior in the office and left approximately forty years later as Managing Director. He married Barbara Bland, who was one of five girls starting the High School from Tower Road

111

School in 1944 and they now both enjoy a retirement, enriched by golf and caravanning. Barbara's father was Harold Bland, who opened bat for Boston Cricket Club for many years.

Peter Day was the sportsman: he played centre forward for the Grammar School first team and was the opening bowler for the first eleven. He was really fast and often skittled the opposing team out, before a bowling change was neccessary. He was tall and dark and naturally attracted the girls; a quirk of fate of which he took full advantage. There must be many today, who remember him with affection, in spite of his determination to play the field. On a Sunday afternoon the regular routine was to walk round the town and through the park and many a time some blushing girl would approach Peter and attempt to arrange an assignation for her friend.

He was an enthusiastic record collector and, although the top twenty had not been thought of, he always knew which record would be the next hit. I remember him playing Red Ingle records, before I had ever heard of him and he was singing "Nature Boy" weeks before it became so popular. He went to work for De Havillands at Hatfield and we have not met since but Noel has kept in touch with him.

Victor Emery was the scientist. He gained a post at the University of California and called in our shop in the early sixties, when he took the opportunity of visiting his parents, while en route to Moscow to deliver a series of lectures. He married a nurse, who lived at Leverton but I heard no further news of them, until Mr. Colin Smith of Swineshead kindly phoned me, after I had mentioned Victor in my column, and told me his son, Graham, had a tenure at the Brookhaven National Laboratory at Long Island, New York and he had met Victor there.

When Graham Smith later went to a conference at Grenoble, he came to England and phoned me from his father's house and explained that Victor was very highly thought of at Brookhaven, where he is rated among the top hundred physicists in the United States. His work is theoretical and he is a leading authority on super conductivity. He assured me that he and his family were fit and well and promised to relay my regards and best wishes.

Although dedicated to his studies at school, Vic still found time for his favourite sport; swimming. He was a well-built lad and very fast in the water: he won the mile race down the Witham each year he entered. Just after the war this race attracted quite a crowd both sides of the river and swimmers came from quite a distance but, as with many former events, it is now just a memory. He also was an important member of the successful Boston Town water polo team.

So to sum up: Noel Holgate was the musician, Peter Day was the sportsman, Victor Emery was the scientist but what was I? I was the organiser; the secretary and treasurer combined; the one who arranged the football and cricket fixtures and made sure the team and the equipment were there on time.

I received my training for this post early, helping my father plan the local bakers' meetings by addresing the postcards that he sent out at regular intervals.

To raise funds I became involved in various activities, all of which proved to be useful training for a budding entrepreneur, a word by the way that was not in use at that time. I sold American comics, most of them begged from my cousin's boy friend; I traded in foreign stamps, buying in bulk and breaking them down into different countries and special sets; I bought a job lot of ladies buttons and mother let me sell them on a small counter in the shop. The net result was that we were never without a football in the winter nor without batting pads in the summer.

So we had a clubroom and we had forty members; now we needed a name. We were determined that all our

Christian names would be contained in the club's name but the best suggestion was Penopauvics. PE for Peter, NO for Noel, PAU for Paul and VIC for Victor. We discarded this idea, when we realised lads in other clubs would never be able to tell their parents who they were playing against and, if they did manage to pronounce it, their parents would worry, thinking they were up against a tribe of red indians.

We turned our attentions then to surnames and so the Demon Sports Club was born. D for Day, EM for Emery, MO for Mould but we had to use N for Noel, as we could find no suitable alternative using a H for Holgate. With plenty to chose from we had both a good football team and a respectable cricket team: we did not lose many games.

There was a surfeit of forwards: Peter Day of course played centre forward and Noel was on the left wing, Gordon Upsall was a very tricky inside forward and Peter Loveley was a regular in the attack. Victor Emery and myself were full backs, Ray Woods was also a defender and Arthur Holamby was a busy half back. Alan Williams played in goal but he was also a useful winger.

We arranged games with various teams: it was about that time that the Unicorn team was started but our most important fixtures were always against Wyberton Rangers. Bryn Johnson and Tommy Horn ran their team and I remember Tony Farrow played for them. It was always close and usually there was only one goal in it or the match was drawn.

One winter I arranged a match with Winthorpe Olympic, who played outside Skegness on the Lincoln Road. We drew 4-4 but I played left back and all four of their goals were scored by the right winger. He was the first coloured player I had marked and he was like greased lightning; I just could not catch him. I heard later he had joined a league club, so I did not feel so bad.

In summer we played our cricket games in the Central

Park. Opposing teams were few but we had several good matches against Sherwood Boys. Their clubroom was in Field Street and it was run for years by Mr. Norman, whose son Alan opened the batting. Just as our attack relied on Peter Day's fast bowling, so they had John Tilling, another celebrated speed merchant.

One particular match sticks in my mind, for during it I gained an unwarranted reputation for being a brilliant close fielder. We had batted first and scored about a hundred, which would normally be enough to win, but, after Peter had disposed of their first four batsmen, Frank Sargeant started hitting nearly every ball through mid-wicket to the boundary. In desperation Peter asked me to field at short leg to close the gap and like a fool I did.

Sure enough Frank hit the next ball like a rocket straight at me. I had no time to avoid it and to protect my teeth I put my hands up and caught it. I was an instant hero and with Frank out they collapsed and we won the match but I never really enjoyed cricket afterwards, because they always expected me to field close to the wicket.

Frank became the Dean of Bradford, then the Bishop of Stockport and he is now the Bishop of Lambeth, helping with the affairs of the Archbishop of Canterbury. While he was the Bishop of Stockport, he had occasion to write to the Head of the North Western Water Board to complain. When his complaint reached the appropriate office the secretary asked the Head of the Water Board what was the correct way to address the Bishop in the reply. He told her he would deal with it personally and started his letter: "Dear Frank,". The Head of the North Western Water Board was none other than Graham Alexander, who had been a classmate and friend of Frank's, when they were at Boston Grammar School.

The Demon Sports Club disbanded, when Peter and Noel became more interested in chasing girls instead of footballs and Victor concentrated on his swimming and water polo. I was left to plough a lone furrow but I soon joined the Mens' Own Club for snooker and table tennis and ran the Old Boys Youth team with Derek Whelbourn and Alan Woodthorpe, representing the team at meetings of the Youth League, which were held in Derek Killick's barbers shop under the chairmanship of Mr. Sewell, the Headmaster of Amber Hill school.

When Mr. Haslam came to teach English at the Grammar School, he brought with him several innovations. He persuaded Mr. Waddams that the school should have a Combined Cadet Force, which he commanded, as he had been a Captain in the Army. I joined and later, when I served my two years National Service in the R.A.F., I blessed Capt. Haslam for helping me to become a marksman and obtain my Cert A, for it enabled me to be upflighted and I only had to survive five weeks square-bashing, instead of eight.

Another idea of Mr. Haslam was for every boy in the class to write a poem about Boston and those good enough would be printed in an anthology. He hoped no doubt for some sonnets or at least an example of iambic pentameter but we knew our limitations and most of us were satisfied to attempt rhyming couplets.

I still have a copy of the five that he considered the best of a disappointing lot and a strange fact is that three of the five were written by boys on the science stream of the class and only two from the arts side.

At the risk of boring you I will include the three shortest poems.

Each Wednesday and each Saturday
The market comes to town
And busy shoppers make their way
To spend their husband's hard-earned pay

With many a sigh and frown.

But all the people do not sigh,
For farmers selling sheep
And cows make pounds; enough to buy
The seeds for barley, wheat and rye,
Which year by year they reap.

At last the day comes to an end;
All business now is done.
The stalls close down and people spend
The night indoors or with a friend
At the pictures, having fun.

V. EMERY

Proudly rising over Boston
Is a church of wide renown
Called, by nickname, "Boston Stump"
In Boston town.

Although we are a little small
And have some baths half-fallen down,
We have a park and library
In Boston town.

We have an ancient Grammar School,
Given to Boston by the Crown,
Which was before a monastery
In Boston town.

J.F. CAMMACK

Standing near the Witham,
Dark against the sky,
The old grey tower of Boston Stump
Uplifts it's head on high.

The houses cluster round it,
Like chicks around a hen.
The river flows beneath the bridge
 Towards the sea again.

It passes by the harbour,
Where men work hard all day
Unloading precious cargoes
Without the least delay.
                    P. MOULD

Today teachers moan about the size of the class and the
shortage of funds for computers and other modern aids.
There was no time wasted in complaining in 1944 by the
emergency lady teachers and those men brought out of
retirement, although there was a desperate shortage of
basic materials; exercise books, pens and pencils; they
just did the best they could with what was available.

Our class never suffered as a consequence, because,
when we took our School Certificate in 1949, we achieved
one of the best batch of results ever recorded; we nearly all
metriculated and we have much to thank our motley medley
of teachers for with their sesquipedalian verbiage and in
some cases their tatterdemalion gowns.

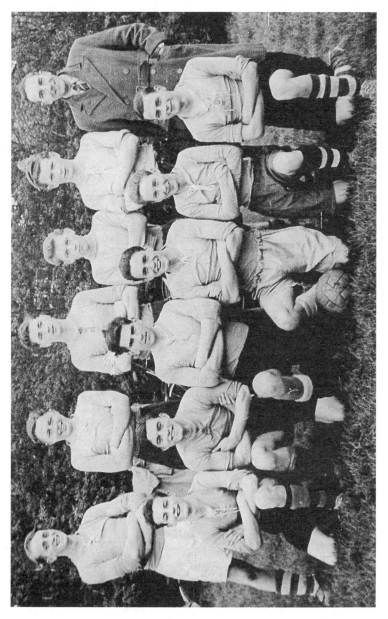

Old Bostonians Youth Team 1949

Back Row (left to right): Dick Parker, Paul Mould, Chuck Virgin, Brian Cocks, Bryn Woodcock, Mr. Alf Read.
Front Row ((left to right): Derek Whelbourn, Alan Woodthorpe, Dick Parkinson, Peter Day, Noel Holgate, Frank Sargeant.

119

SEE YOU AT JIMMIES!

Throughout the war and for many years after the most popular meeting place for Grammar School boys and High School girls was Jimmy Ward's herbal store. When a tryst was being arranged, it was the first venue to be mentioned. Young lads, who had neither the money nor the nerve to buy cigarettes, were often introduced to the pleasures of smoking by Jimmy's much cheaper and safer herbal smoking mixture. When they bought a clay pipe, their parents innocently thought they were planning to blow bubbles.

His shop was only small but often over twenty crammed inside with in the summer an overspill of another ten enjoying their drinks outside. In his glory years he traded opposite Cheers, between the Co-op and Forinton's furniture shop and there was a small area, where you could stand without blocking the pavement.

The colourful barrels on his shelf held the magic elixirs that transformed a glass of water into a mouth-watering variety of flavours: Cherry, Orange, Blackcurrant, Lemon, or Sasparella. They could all be bought cold or hot. If you had a cold or if you were trying to impress the girls of your manhood, you ordered a hot compo and drank it straight down, even if it nearly burned your throat.

Dick Parkinson recalled regularly reviving himself with a hot sasparella, after a vigorous session in the nets, followed by a hour of fielding practise. Dick was in my brother's class and lived at the top of Woodville Road near the playing field. In those days there were many more shrubs and small trees around the field and it was an ideal site to play "thrasher".

With Johnny Smith, who lived in Westfield Avenue, he persuaded a group of friends, including my brother, to risk life and limb and join them in a game. Jim, my brother, used to take me along to make up the numbers; the more the merrier.

For the uninitiated "thrasher" was an advanced form of "tiggy". Depending on how many were playing, either one or two had to prevent everyone else from reaching safety, after they had used the time taken counting a hundred to hide in the shrubs. The difference was that, instead of just tigging (touching) the person, you had to hit them with a thrown missile, which in our case was usually a hardened brussel sprout stalk, long shorn of it's brussels.

If you were hit, you had to take your turn at being the "thrasher". The art of the game was to dash for home, while they were chasing some other unfortunate and, if you were spotted, wait until the missile was in flight, before taking diversionary action.

The danger came, if you were hit in the face, the kidneys or any other tender area but, as I was the smallest participant, I had the obvious advantage of being a smaller target and could hide in smaller bushes.

John Crabb also had happy memories of Jimmy Ward's emporium, which he first visited, when he started to work
as an errand boy at Forinton's furniture shop. He became one of Jimmy's "boys", who received with their drinks nuggets of advice, which, if heeded, stood them in good stead in later life.

Jimmy's wife sometimes helped or took over, while he had a meal or a well-earned rest. The position at the right-hand extremity of the counter was almost always occupied by Jimmy's constant companion, whose function seemed to be to endorse everything Jimmy said and grin broadly at every anecdote Jimmy delivered. He rarely presumed to join in the actual conversation but, if absent, Jimmy's witticisms did not carry so much conviction.

His name was Ralph and at one time I believe he had

worked for the corporation. He lived down Norfolk Place with his aunt, Mrs. Damms, a genuine, kind lady, who appreciated his help around the house and raised no objection to his extended visits to Jimmy's.

G.I. BRIDE

On 7th. February,1945 my cousin, Leila Rastall, joined the thousands of British girls, who became G.I. Brides. She married Lloyd Lewis, an American airman, whose parents owned a ten pin bowling alley in a small town on the Californian coast.

We had moved in November, 1944 from the sweet and cigarette shop at 108, High Street to 65, High Street, a much larger house with numerous rooms. When Leila asked my mother, if she could have her wedding reception at our house, she was pleased to oblige.

Leila's father, Bart Rastall, who was a milkman, had died, while she was young, so her mother's brother, Ernest Blackamore, whom we all called "Uncle Blackie", gave her away. Leila's younger sister, Thora and a friend in the WAAFs were her attendants.

Several of Lloyd's friends came to the reception but I only remember his best man, because he stood out with his bright ginger hair and he was appropriately known as Red Horn.

Leila had left the High School, after taking her School Certificate in 1940 and worked at the County Hall for two years. At eighteen she had joined the Land Army for a while, then joined the WAAFs.

We had already met Lloyd, for Leila felt close to my mother, her "Auntie Cissy" and, while still at the High School, she had kept my father's accounts in order, so she had spent a lot of time with us and she brought Lloyd to tea once or twice on Sundays before the wedding.

I became very friendly with Lloyd and, as I mentioned earlier, he supplied me with numerous American comics, which I read quickly and passed on to my classmates very profitably.

Soon after the wedding Lloyd was posted to Georgetown

in British Guiana, where he met an American soldier called Harry Findon. During their conversation Harry mentioned that he had a friend back home in the United States, who was a keen philatelist and enjoyed corresponding with collectors in other countries. Lloyd gave him my name and address and in August, 1945 I received my first letter from Paul Fulton Bair.

This friend of Harry Findon was aged 31 and had contracted Infantile Paralysis, when he was three, leaving him paralised in both legs and confined to a wheelchair. He lived at the Saint Barnabas Free Home in Gibsonia, Allegheny County, Pennsylvania, which was nineteen miles from Pittsburg.

The Home was for incurable men and boys and Paul Fulton Bair ran the entire office, while the regular staff were away at war. There were 107 patients, so he was kept busy. His mother, father and elder brother were all dead, so the Home was his whole life and he gained immense pleasure from receiving letters from a girl in South Africa and two gentlemen in New Zealand. He was delighted to add my name to his list of pen friends.

He managed to play Billiards and table tennis from his wheelchair but his favourite game was chess, which did not take so much out of him. Much of his spare time was spent in his stamp collecting and he sent me a selection of U.S. commemoratives with every letter.

One day in March, 1946 I came home from school and my mother said a wooden box had arrived for me from America. The lid was screwed down and it took me a while to open it. I could see from the postmark it was from Pennsylvania and I guessed it was a stamp album but why such a big box?

It certainly was an album; the biggest, most detailed album you could imagine. It was fully bound and there was a space in it for every stamp that had been issued up to

1940. In his next letter Paul said he hoped it was not too big for me but it was the only size available, until things returned to normal, as paper was needed for more urgent usage. He assured me that he would sent the pages for stamps issued after 1940, as soon as they were printed.

It must have cost a lot of money but he would not let me send anything towards the expense of either the album or the postage. The top of the box was covered in stamps.

In return I sent him the few stamps that were issued for Great Britain but at that time they were few and far between; not like today, when new sets are released at every possible occasion. I also sent him some photographs and he was very pleased with them and afterwards in every letter he asked after my whole family.

He also wrote regularly to Leila, until March, 1946, when she sailed to America to join up with Lloyd, who had just been demobbed from the U.S. Air Force.

His letters were always interesting and they gave me an idea of what life was like in Pittsburg towards the end of the war and just after. The only thing rationed in America was sugar, although many things were scarce.

In the spring of 1946 all America was hit by strikes; one of the complications of the immediate post-war period. Everybody over there seemed to be worried about the possibility of war with Russia and hoped that the conflict would be settled quickly, because, as Paul said, "the whole world needs peace."

Paul sent me photographs of himself and the Saint Barnabas Free Home, as it was in summer and winter. He organised games of softball against other homes in the winter and baseball in the summer. In a letter he wrote on 28th. August, 1946 he expressed a hope that we may meet some day, if I was ever able to visit Leila, who by then was settled in California.

In his last paragraph he said he had suffered a bout of flu and they had been concerned at the Home in case it should develope into pneumonia. My next two letters were never answered and eventually I had to accept that he failed to recover from his illness, for from his photographs I could see he was very frail and would not be able to resist pneumonia.

My sister kept in touch with Leila over the years and also her sister, Thora, who emigrated to Canada. Thora unfortunately died about twelve years ago but she came back for a holiday and we met her husband and three children. Leila never returned to England and she lost her husband but she lives happily with her son, Jimbo, higher up the west coast at Gold Beech, Oregon and she has a daughter, who lives in New York.

With her son in the summer she travels to the State Fairs and sells Mexican antiques, then Jimbo has a trip to Mexico during the winter to replenish their stock, while Leila has a kiosk in a local shop. I receive a letter from her every Christmas and another around Easter, before she starts her summer trips.

Leila Rastall marries Lloyd Lewis

8TH. MAY, 1945

Winston Churchill made the official announcement that the war in Europe was over at 3.00 p.m. on Tuesday, 8th. May, 1945. Simultaneous announcements were made in Washington and Moscow. Later at 9.00 p.m. the King spoke to Great Britain and the Empire on the radio.

A group of six German Generals and Admirals had surrendered to Field Marshall Montgomery at Luneburg Heath.

The whole country was given a two-day holiday but there was not time to organise street parties, so most of these were held the following week-end.

In Boston Pop Norman arranged a memorable party at the Sherwood Youth Club in Field Street and music was provided by their own band with Bob Kitchen on piano, "Scorcher" Porcher on the drums, "Mousey" Hall on double base and Melvyn Franklin on piano accordian.

The May Fair was in town and it was allowed to stay for an extra week. Mr. Harold Kemp recorded the scene for posterity by painting a view of Bargate Green on V.E. Day, featuring the popular Moon Rocket ride. The bunting seen round the perimeter of the Green was repeated all over town. The landlord of the Vine public house in Broadfield Street had a flash of inspiration and made a large sign for his window that read V in E.

Some people did not join in the festivities wholeheartedly, although they were naturally pleased but several families still had loved ones fighting against the Japanese in Burma and the Far East. For them the celebrations could not start in earnest, until 8.00 a.m. on Wednesday, 15th. August, when it was announced on the radio that Japan had surrendered.

The Wednesday and Thursday were declared a public holiday and huge bonfires were built all over the country. In Boston Mr. Harold Kemp again positioned himself

137

somewhere near the top of Threadneedle Street and painted the same scene as on 8th. May but this time he showed the hugh crowds rejoicing around a massive bonfire in the centre of Bargate Green with Cammack's furniture store prominent on the skyline.

The more nimble and adventurous in the crowd climbed on top of the air-raid shelters on two sides of the Green and joined in with the singing and dancing from their elevated position. One gentleman in his sixties had been celebrating all day but still managed to reach the top of a shelter, where he gave a spirited demonstration of the sailors' hornpipe to his younger companions. He lost his footing and fell but suffered no ill effects and just stood up and carried on with his exhibition.

The previous Monday I had accompanied my mother and sister to Lincoln to visit my mother's cousin, who lived above the Co-operative Store at the top of King Street. We left my father and my sister's boy friend, Johnny Colam, puling the pears off the giant tree behind our house at 65, High Street.

On the Monday night we went to the Savoy cinema and saw Gregory Peck in "The Keys Of The Kingdom" and between the films an organist appeared out of the floor playing the latest tunes. At the time this impressed me more than the film, for we had nothing like this in Boston.

We went to the Theatre Royal on the Tuesday night, where Syd Makin was featured in a revue "Makin Hey!, While The Sun Shines". It was probably as bad as it sounds from the weak pun in the name of the show but it was a new experience for me and I told my brother in a letter that I enjoyed it.

After the announcement on the Wednesday morning, the rest of our plans were forgotten and we joined thousands of people on the Wednesday evening dancing in Portland Street, the next turning off High Street after King Street.

My brother was not with us, because he had gone to Hitchingbrook Park in Huntingdon with Skip Lucas and the Fifth Boston Scout Troop. They were at summer camp and on the Wednesday evening they took part in a hastily-arranged torchlight parade through the streets of Huntingdon.

POSTSCRIPT

On 8th. June, 1946 every schoolchild received a letter from the King. It read:

"Today, as we celebrate victory, I send this personal message to you and all other boys and girls at school. For you have shared in the hardships and dangers of a total war and you have shared no less in the triumph of the Allied Nations.

I know you will always feel proud to belong to a country, which was capable of such supreme effort; proud too of parents and elder brothers and sisters, who by their courage, endurance and enterprise brought victory. May these qualities be yours as you grow up and join in the common effort to establish among the nations of the world unity and peace."

GEORGE REX

ACKNOWLEDGEMENTS
of help and encouragement

BRENDA AND BURT BADLEY

AUDREY COLAM (SISTER)

JAMES MOULD (BROTHER)

MARGARET ALLGOOD (MADDRELL)

W.K. BARKHAM

GEORGE BELL

PETER BLANCHARD

JOHN CLARK

BERNARD CODD

JOHN CRABB

L.W. CRYER

AUSTIN DAVIES

ROBIN EVERETT

ANN FARMER

DICK GRESSWELL

FRANK HARNESS

YVONNE HIMSWORTH

NOEL HOLGATE

R.D. HUGHES

TONY JAKES

WALT LADDS

PETER LEEBETTER

MARGARET LEE (COX)

146

ACKNOWLEDGEMENTS
continued...

TONY MILLS

IAN MITCHELL

ALICE MOWBRAY

ROY NICHOLS

BARBARA PARKER (MADDISON)

DICK PARKINSON

J. PEPPER

GERALD PLUMMER

MICHAEL PRIESTLEY

G. RAYNER

HAZEL RIMINGTON

RON RUSKIN

R. SCALES

RUTH SIMPSON

GRAHAM SMITH

MICHELE WILLIS (STEVENS)

REG WAKEFIELD

PAT WESTLAND

JIM WIGHTMAN

RAY WOODS

CHARLES WRIGHT

NIGEL WAINWRIGHT